Magical History Tour™

3 in 1 3

Collecting "Gandhi"
"The Vikings" and "The Titanic"

FABRICE ERRE
Writer

SYLVAIN SAVOIA
Artist

Magical History Tour™

3 in 1 3

Collecting "Gandhi" "The Vikings" and "The Titanic"

By Fabrice Erre and Sylvain Savoia

Original series editors: Frédéric Niffle and Lewis Trondheim
Color Prep: Luc Perdriset
English Translations by Nanette McGuinness
"Gandhi" and "The Vikings" lettering by Jeff Whitman
"The Titanic" lettering by Wilson Ramos Jr.

Juan Diego Posada — *Production*
Jordan Hillman and Ingrid Rios — *Original Editorial Interns*
Jeff Whitman — *Original Managing Editor*
Stephanie Brooks — *Editor*
Mike Marts — *Editor-in-Chief*

Papercutz was founded by Terry Nantier and Jim Salicrup.

www.papercutz.com

January 2025
Printed in China
First Printing

ISBN 978-1-5458-1837-4

FABRICE ERRE • SYLVAIN SAVOIA

Magical History Tour™

NICO

ANNIE

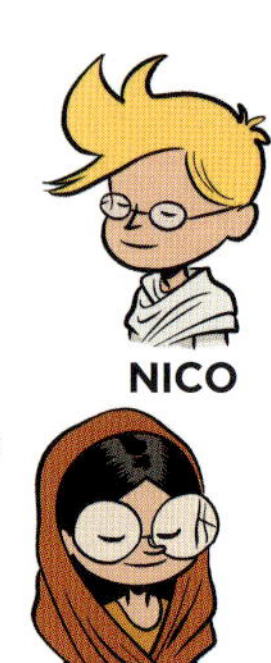

Gandhi
Soldier of Peace

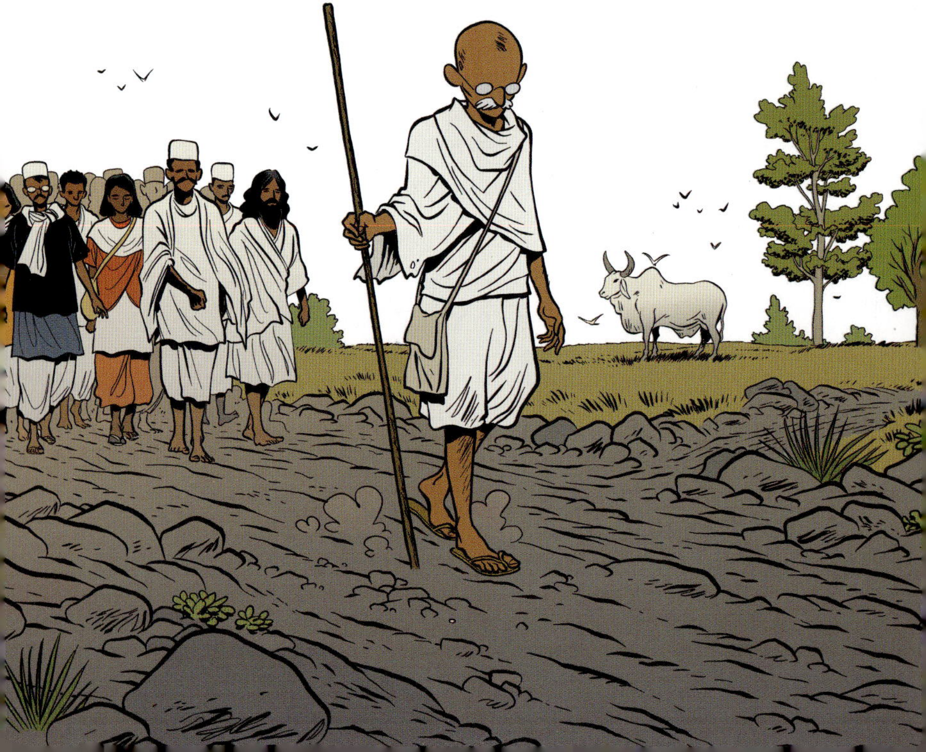

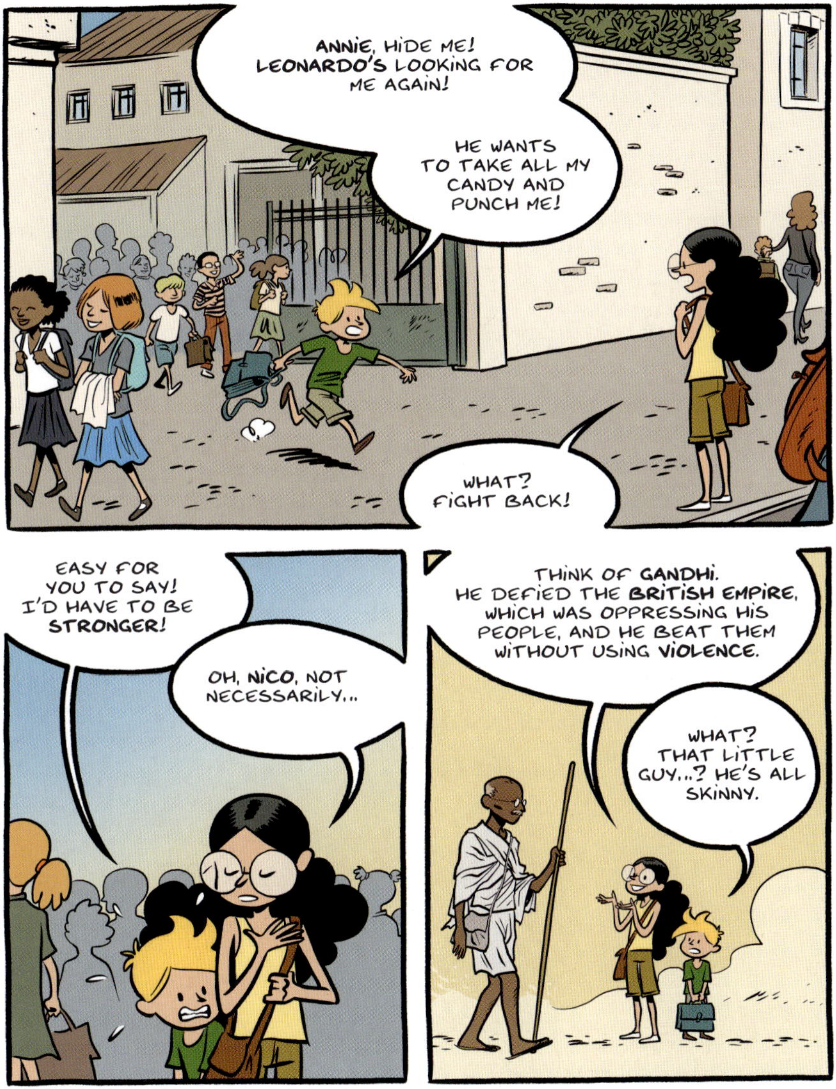

ANNIE, HIDE ME! LEONARDO'S LOOKING FOR ME AGAIN!
HE WANTS TO TAKE ALL MY CANDY AND PUNCH ME!
WHAT? FIGHT BACK!

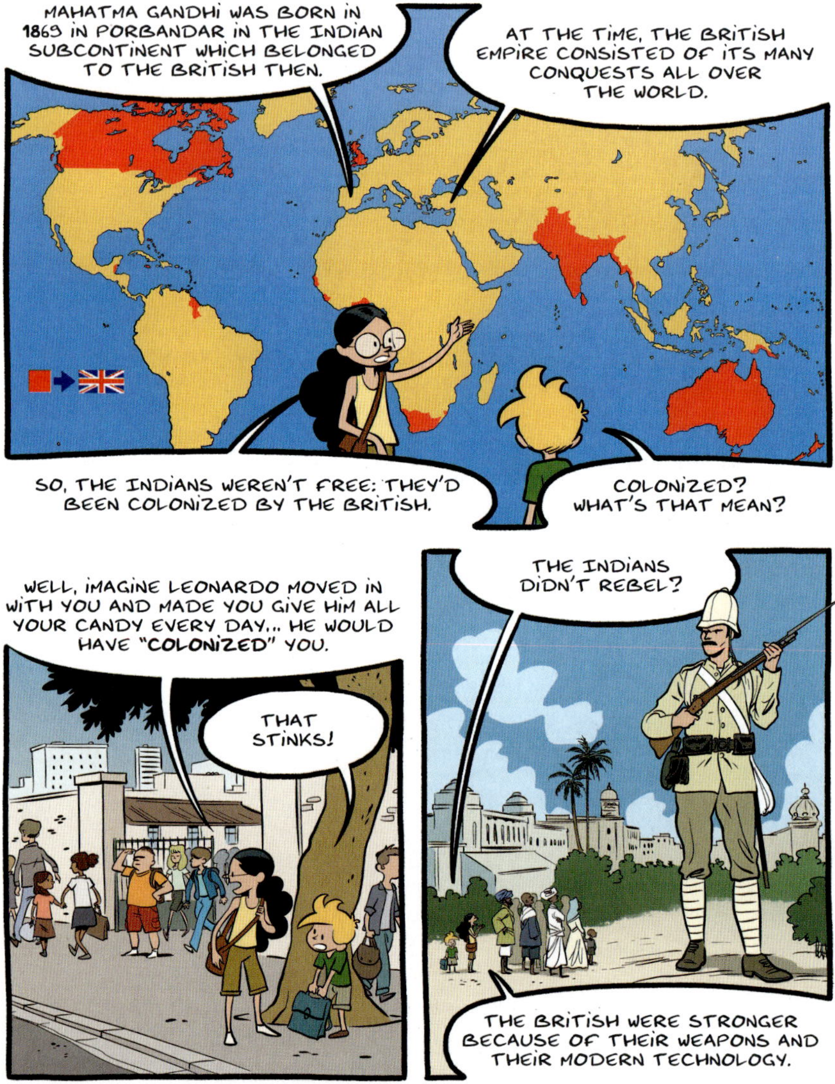

MAHATMA GANDHI WAS BORN IN 1869 IN PORBANDAR IN THE INDIAN SUBCONTINENT WHICH BELONGED TO THE BRITISH THEN.

AT THE TIME, THE BRITISH EMPIRE CONSISTED OF ITS MANY CONQUESTS ALL OVER THE WORLD.

SO, THE INDIANS WEREN'T FREE: THEY'D BEEN COLONIZED BY THE BRITISH.

COLONIZED? WHAT'S THAT MEAN?

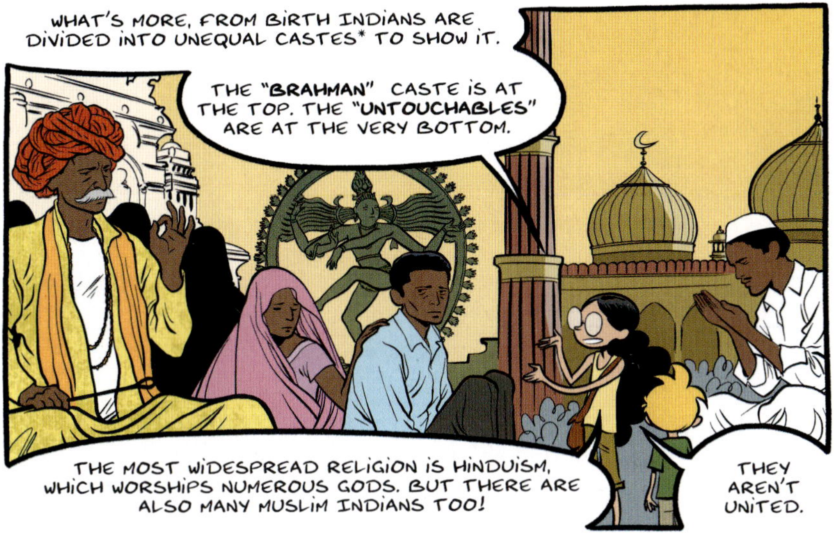

WHAT'S MORE, FROM BIRTH INDIANS ARE DIVIDED INTO UNEQUAL CASTES* TO SHOW IT.

THE "**BRAHMAN**" CASTE IS AT THE TOP. THE "**UNTOUCHABLES**" ARE AT THE VERY BOTTOM.

THE MOST WIDESPREAD RELIGION IS HINDUISM, WHICH WORSHIPS NUMEROUS GODS. BUT THERE ARE ALSO MANY MUSLIM INDIANS TOO!

THEY AREN'T UNITED.

GANDHI WAS BORN INTO A MIDDLE CASTE–A MERCHANT CASTE–TO A HINDU FAMILY.

*DIFFERENT GROUPS THAT DON'T INTERMINGLE.

HE HAD A HAPPY CHILDHOOD, ALTHOUGH SHORT, BUT THE START OF HIS ADULT LIFE WAS HARD.

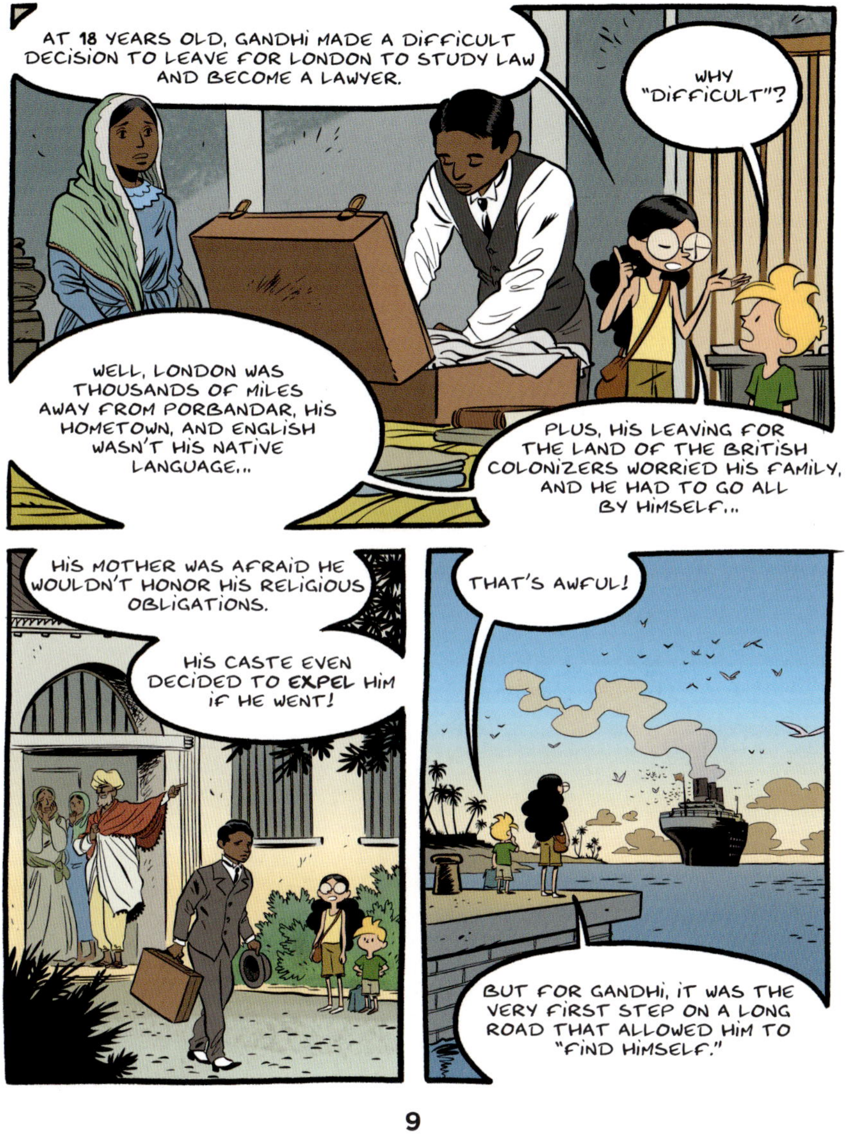

AT 18 YEARS OLD, GANDHI MADE A DIFFICULT DECISION TO LEAVE FOR LONDON TO STUDY LAW AND BECOME A LAWYER.

WHY "DIFFICULT"?

WELL, LONDON WAS THOUSANDS OF MILES AWAY FROM PORBANDAR, HIS HOMETOWN, AND ENGLISH WASN'T HIS NATIVE LANGUAGE...

PLUS, HIS LEAVING FOR THE LAND OF THE BRITISH COLONIZERS WORRIED HIS FAMILY, AND HE HAD TO GO ALL BY HIMSELF...

WHEN HE ARRIVED, GANDHI WAS READY TO BECOME A "EUROPEANIZED" INDIAN, ONE OF THE "EDUCATED NATIVES" THAT THE BRITISH USED TO LEAD COLONIZED PEOPLES.

EXILED, FAR FROM HIS FAMILY, HE BECAME AWARE OF THE IMPORTANCE OF INDIAN CULTURE. HE BECAME A VEGETARIAN AND GREW MORE INTERESTED IN RELIGIONS.

HE LEARNED FROM HINDUISM THAT WANTING USUALLY LEADS TO SUFFERING AND FIGHTING.

WANTING A PIECE OF CANDY IS A SOURCE OF SUFFERING?
YES, BECAUSE AFTER THAT, YOU'LL WANT ANOTHER, THEN ANOTHER... YOU'LL BE ENSLAVED BY CANDY AND YOU'LL WANT TO TAKE IT FROM OTHERS.

SO, WHEN YOU WANT SOME CANDY, YOU SHOULD MEDITATE AND GET RID OF THE DESIRE.

GANDHI ALSO FOUND INSPIRATION IN ISLAM AND CHRISTIANITY.
FOR HIM, FAITH LED TO PEACE: IF YOU MEDITATE INSTEAD OF FIGHTING, THE WORLD WILL BE BETTER.
BIBLE
KORAN
BHAGAVAD GITA
HMMM... BUT IF LEONARDO COMES TO HIT ME, I CAN'T DEFEND MYSELF BY MEDITATING.
THAT'S WHY GANDHI SEARCHED THROUGHOUT HIS LIFE FOR EFFECTIVE BUT PACIFIST METHODS OF CHANGING THINGS...

THE FIRST OF THESE METHODS, OF COURSE, WAS TO ENFORCE THE LAW. IN 1891, GANDHI FINISHED HIS LEGAL STUDIES AND DECIDED TO GO BACK HOME.

HE'D HAD TROUBLE STARTING HIS CAREER. IT WASN'T SO EASY FINDING CLIENTS AT FIRST.
COULD HE HELP ME WITH LEONARDO? WE COULD PAY HIM WITH CANDY.

IN 1893, HE ACCEPTED AN OFFER FROM AN INDIAN COMPANY TO GO WORK FOR THEM IN SOUTH AFRICA.
WOW! THAT'S FAR!

THE REGION WAS ALSO PART OF THE BRITISH EMPIRE. HE DISCOVERED A LOT OF RACISM THERE.

ALL THESE COMMUNITIES DISTRUSTED EACH OTHER AND OFTEN CLASHED.

GANDHI ARRIVED THERE, CONVINCED HE COULD UPHOLD WHAT WAS RIGHT VIA THE LAW.

BUT HE QUICKLY REALIZED THAT THE LAW WAS MADE BY THE "WHITES"...

A WEEK AFTER HE ARRIVED, GANDHI HAD TO TAKE THE TRAIN.
HIS FIRM HAD PAID FOR A FIRST-CLASS TICKET.

ALONG THE ROUTE, A WHITE PASSENGER COMPLAINED ABOUT SEEING A "COOLIE" IN HIS COMPARTMENT.
WHAT DO YOU MEAN?

THE WHITE COLONISTS DISTRUSTED INDIANS AND BLACKS AND REFUSED TO SHARE THE SAME SPACE WITH THEM.

SO GANDHI WAS KICKED OFF THE TRAIN.
BUT THAT'S NOT FAIR!

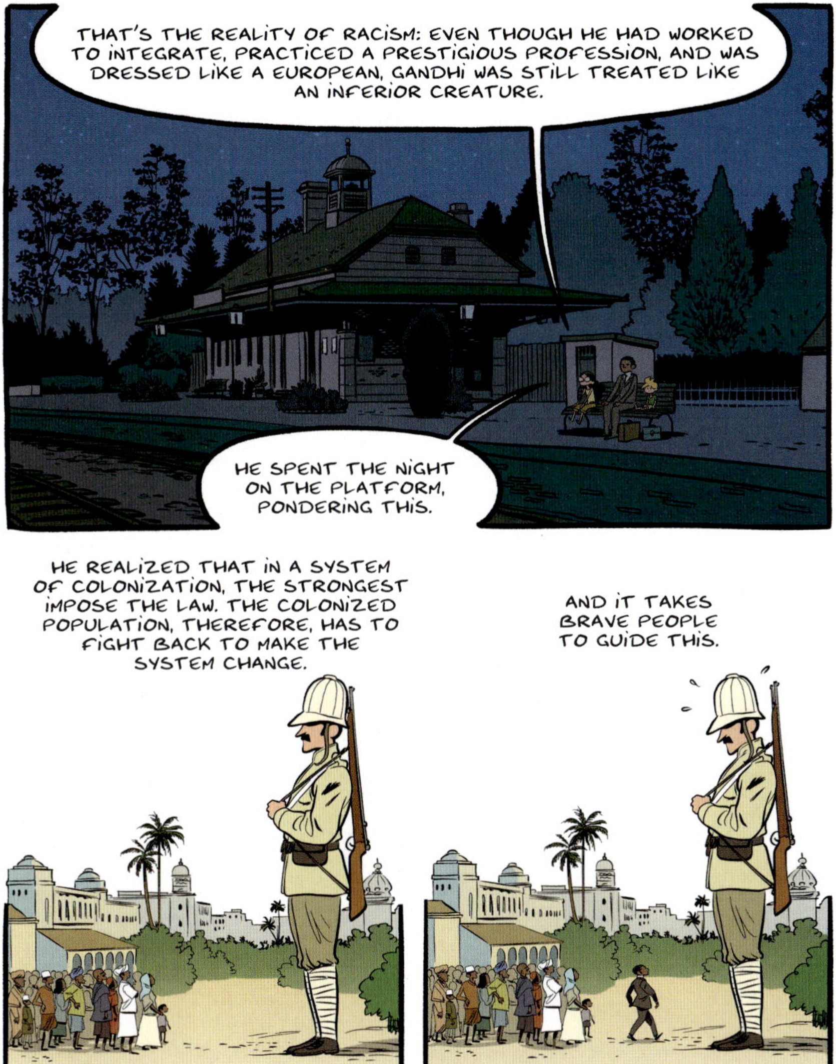

THAT'S THE REALITY OF RACISM: EVEN THOUGH HE HAD WORKED TO INTEGRATE, PRACTICED A PRESTIGIOUS PROFESSION, AND WAS DRESSED LIKE A EUROPEAN, GANDHI WAS STILL TREATED LIKE AN INFERIOR CREATURE.

HE SPENT THE NIGHT ON THE PLATFORM, PONDERING THIS.

HE REALIZED THAT IN A SYSTEM OF COLONIZATION, THE STRONGEST IMPOSE THE LAW. THE COLONIZED POPULATION, THEREFORE, HAS TO FIGHT BACK TO MAKE THE SYSTEM CHANGE.

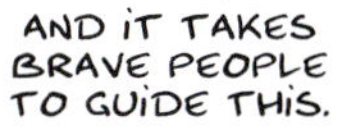

GANDHI BECAME THE SPOKESPERSON FOR INDIANS IN SOUTH AFRICA. HE BEGAN BY GETTING THEM THE RIGHT TO TRAVEL BY TRAIN WHEN THEY WERE PROPERLY DRESSED.
THAT WAS HIS REVENGE!

HE WROTE PETITIONS, FOUNDED A POLITICAL PARTY, WROTE BOOKS, GAVE SPEECHES... HIS POPULARITY QUICKLY GREW.
EQUAL RIGHTS
HE LOOKS LESS SHY ALREADY.

ALL THAT MUST NOT HAVE PLEASED THE COLONISTS.
THAT'S FOR SURE.

IN 1896, HE WENT TO FIND HIS FAMILY IN INDIA. WHEN HE RETURNED TO SOUTH AFRICA, HIS SHIP WAS QUARANTINED IN THE PORT OF DURBAN.
WHY?

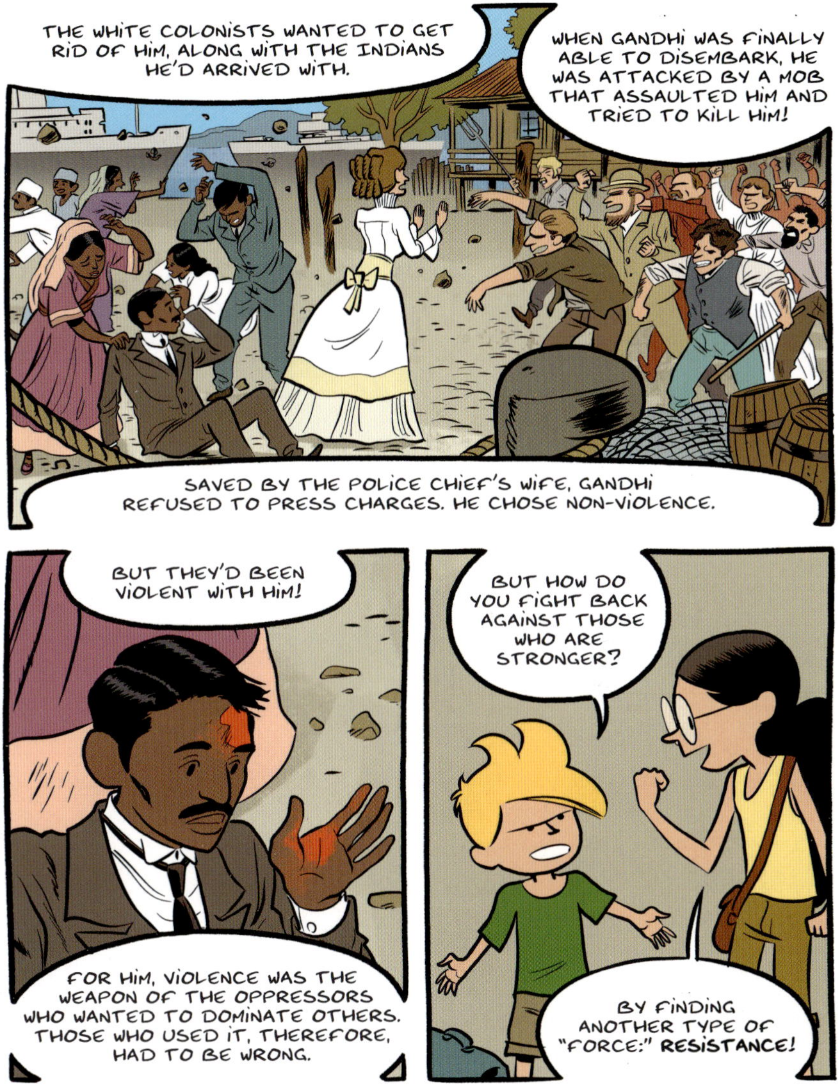

THE WHITE COLONISTS WANTED TO GET RID OF HIM, ALONG WITH THE INDIANS HE'D ARRIVED WITH.

WHEN GANDHI WAS FINALLY ABLE TO DISEMBARK, HE WAS ATTACKED BY A MOB THAT ASSAULTED HIM AND TRIED TO KILL HIM!

SAVED BY THE POLICE CHIEF'S WIFE, GANDHI REFUSED TO PRESS CHARGES. HE CHOSE NON-VIOLENCE.

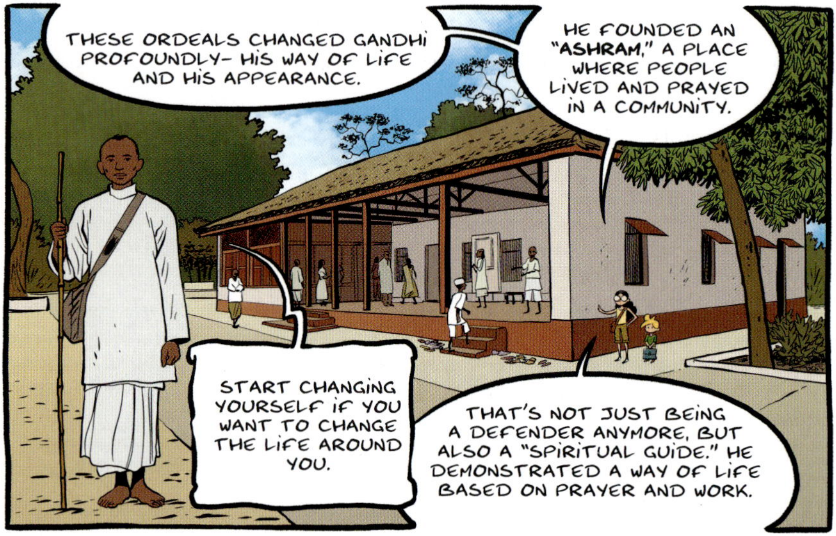

THESE ORDEALS CHANGED GANDHI PROFOUNDLY– HIS WAY OF LIFE AND HIS APPEARANCE.

HE FOUNDED AN "**ASHRAM**," A PLACE WHERE PEOPLE LIVED AND PRAYED IN A COMMUNITY.

START CHANGING YOURSELF IF YOU WANT TO CHANGE THE LIFE AROUND YOU.

THAT'S NOT JUST BEING A DEFENDER ANYMORE, BUT ALSO A "SPIRITUAL GUIDE." HE DEMONSTRATED A WAY OF LIFE BASED ON PRAYER AND WORK.

INDIANS COULD COUNT ON THEIR NUMBERS: IF THEY RESISTED THE BRITISH WITHOUT USING VIOLENCE, THEY WOULD BE ABLE TO SET AN EXAMPLE AND OBTAIN THEIR RIGHTS.

IN 1913, NON-WHITE MARRIAGES WERE DECLARED ILLEGAL AND A TAX WAS IMPOSED ON INDIAN WORKERS. SEVERAL THOUSAND MINERS AND WOMEN DEMONSTRATED PEACEFULLY.

THE BRITISH REACTED VIOLENTLY AND IMPRISONED GANDHI.

FACING THE RESISTANCE OF 50,000 INDIANS ON STRIKE, THE BRITISH WERE FORCED TO YIELD. THEY FREED GANDHI AND CANCELED THESE MEASURES.

AFTER SPENDING 22 YEARS IN SOUTH AFRICA, GANDHI HAD SUCCESSFULLY INVENTED A FORM OF PEACEFUL CONFLICT. SO HE DECIDED TO USE IT IN INDIA.

RETURNING TO HIS NATIVE LAND IN 1915, GANDHI FOUNDED A NEW COMMUNITY IN AHMEDABAD AND TRAVELED TO MEET THE POPULATION.

IN SOUTH AFRICA, HE HAD FOUGHT FOR THE RIGHTS OF HIS COMMUNITY. IN INDIA, HE HAD TO GET READY FOR A MUCH BIGGER FIGHT.

WELL, IT WOULD BE AS IF YOU'D MANAGED TO GET LEONARDO NOT TO EAT YOUR CANDY AND THEN YOU ALSO WANTED HIM TO LEAVE YOUR HOUSE.

GANDHI EXPLAINED IN A BOOK THAT INDIANS HAD TO FIGHT FOR THEIR RIGHTS AND ALSO GAIN THEIR INDEPENDENCE–GET RID OF THE BRITISH!

HE MET THOSE WHO HAD ALREADY BEEN FIGHTING FOR THIS FOR MANY YEARS.
ANNIE BESANT, AN ENGLISHWOMAN WHO HAD MOVED TO INDIA TO HELP FREE IT.
EVEN THOUGH SHE WAS BRITISH?
JAWAHARLAL NEHRU, SON OF THE PRESIDENT OF THE INDIAN NATIONAL CONGRESS, WHO FOUGHT FOR INDIANS' POLITICAL RIGHTS.
WELL, YES!
RABINDRANATH TAGORE, AN INDIAN PHILOSOPHER, WHO NICKNAMED GANDHI "MAHATMA," I.E., "GREAT SOUL."
GANDHI WAS READY TO LEAD A COLLECTIVE FIGHT. IN 1921, HE WAS ELECTED PRESIDENT OF THE INDIAN NATIONAL CONGRESS AND PLANNED TO FOLLOW HIS OWN METHODS.

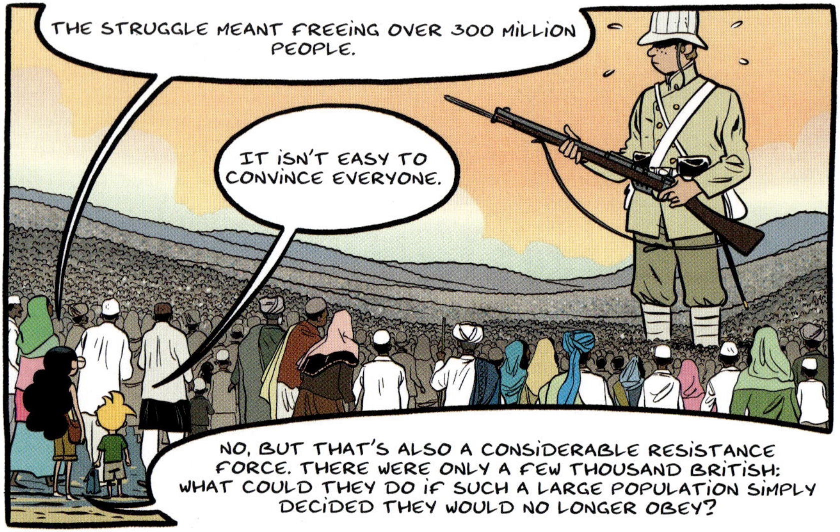

THE STRUGGLE MEANT FREEING OVER 300 MILLION PEOPLE.

IT ISN'T EASY TO CONVINCE EVERYONE.

NO, BUT THAT'S ALSO A CONSIDERABLE RESISTANCE FORCE. THERE WERE ONLY A FEW THOUSAND BRITISH: WHAT COULD THEY DO IF SUCH A LARGE POPULATION SIMPLY DECIDED THEY WOULD NO LONGER OBEY?

GANDHI INVENTED THREE METHODS OF "**CIVIL DISOBEDIENCE**," WHICH ANYONE COULD IMPLEMENT, AND WHICH COULD BE DONE COLLECTIVELY.

* HARTAL MEANS STRIKE IN HINDI.

FOR GANDHI, IT WAS A WAY TO PUT PRESSURE ON AN OPPONENT, WHO BECAME RESPONSIBLE FOR LETTING THE FASTING PERSON DIE. IT WAS ALSO A WAY TO "PURIFY" THE BODY.

AND DID IT WORK?

NOT EVERY TIME, NOT RIGHT AWAY...

IT WAS A LONG ROAD AND TENSION GREW IN INDIA...

EVEN THOUGH GANDHI LEAD BY EXAMPLE, UNCONTROL-LABLE VIOLENCE SOMETIMES BROKE OUT.

ON APRIL 13, 1919, IN AMRITSAR, BRITISH POLICE FIRED ON INDIANS WHO HAD GATHERED PEACEFULLY. THE SLAUGHTER LASTED TEN MINUTES AND LEFT 379 DEAD AND ABOUT 1200 WOUNDED.

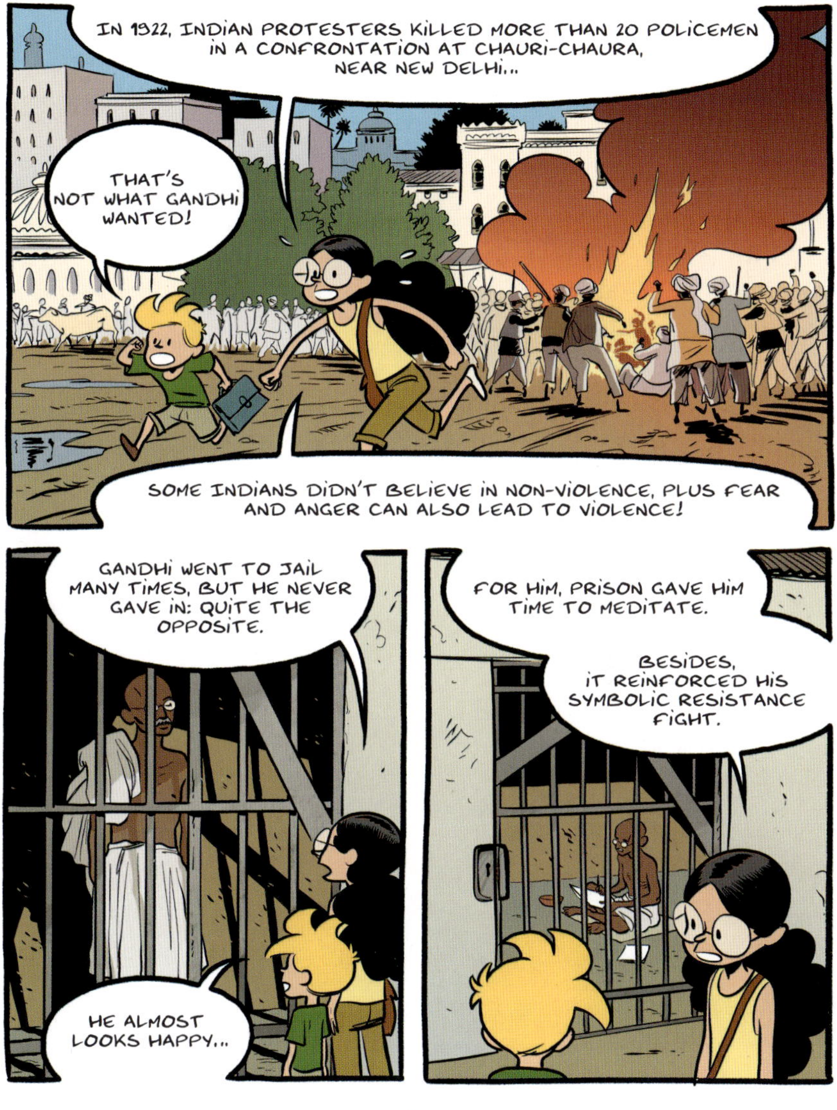

IN 1922, INDIAN PROTESTERS KILLED MORE THAN 20 POLICEMEN IN A CONFRONTATION AT CHAURI-CHAURA, NEAR NEW DELHI...

THAT'S NOT WHAT GANDHI WANTED!

SOME INDIANS DIDN'T BELIEVE IN NON-VIOLENCE, PLUS FEAR AND ANGER CAN ALSO LEAD TO VIOLENCE!

IN A PEACEFUL FIGHT, A SYMBOL IS IMPORTANT: IT BRINGS PEOPLE TOGETHER AND GIVES THEM A SHARED IMAGE.
GANDHI, HIMSELF, BECAME A **SYMBOL**.
HE WROTE A LOT AND LIVED IN POVERTY. IT WAS SAID THAT HE ONLY OWNED HIS CLOTHES, HIS GLASSES, AND THREE MONKEY FIGURINES...

WHAT IS THAT THING?
IT'S A SPINNING WHEEL FOR COTTON, ANOTHER SYMBOL: GANDHI WANTED TO ENCOURAGE INDIANS TO MAKE THEIR OWN FABRIC INSTEAD OF BUYING IT FROM THE BRITISH.
WHETHER GANDHI WORKED, PRAYED, FASTED, OR WAS IN JAIL, HIS BEHAVIOR BECAME A MODEL THAT THE INDIAN PEOPLE FOLLOWED AND RESPECTED.

IN MARCH 1930, HE LAUNCHED A MAJOR SYMBOLIC CAMPAIGN: **THE SALT MARCH.**
IN INDIA, THE BRITISH CONTROLLED SALT PRODUCTION. INDIANS WERE FORBIDDEN TO HARVEST IT THEMSELVES. GANDHI CHALLENGED THIS LAW AND ASSEMBLED A GROUP OF DEMONSTRATORS TO MAKE THE 240-MILE TRIP TO THE SEA.
WHEN HE ARRIVED AT THE BEACH, GANDHI GATHERED A HANDFUL OF SALT. IN THIS WAY, HE SYMBOLICALLY SHOWED THAT SALT BELONGS TO EVERYONE.
THE MARCH WAS A HUGE SUCCESS!
AND DID THE BRITISH THROW GANDHI INTO JAIL AFTER THE MARCH?
YES, FOR NINE MONTHS! ALONG WITH 60,000 OTHERS! BUT THE SYMBOL REMAINED.
THE FIST WHICH HELD THE SALT MAY BE BROKEN, BUT IT WILL NOT YIELD UP ITS SALT.

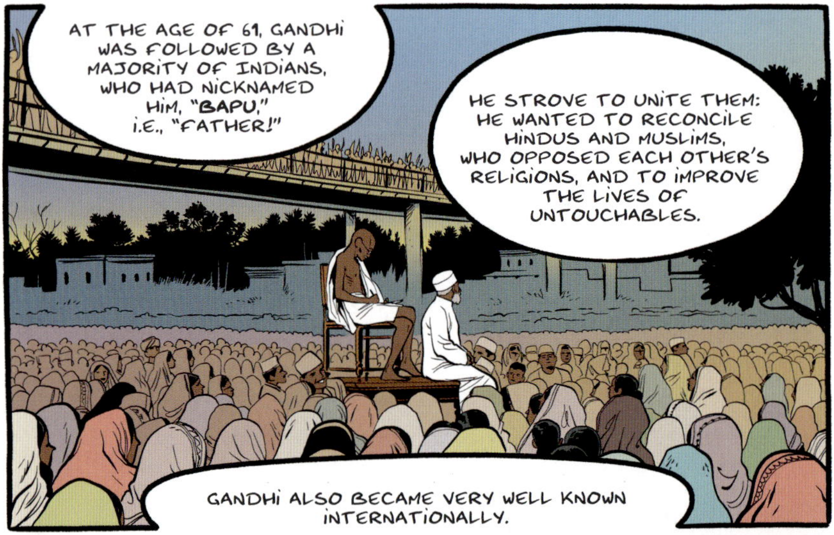

AT THE AGE OF 61, GANDHI WAS FOLLOWED BY A MAJORITY OF INDIANS, WHO HAD NICKNAMED HIM, "**BAPU**," I.E., "FATHER!"

HE STROVE TO UNITE THEM: HE WANTED TO RECONCILE HINDUS AND MUSLIMS, WHO OPPOSED EACH OTHER'S RELIGIONS, AND TO IMPROVE THE LIVES OF UNTOUCHABLES.

GANDHI ALSO BECAME VERY WELL KNOWN INTERNATIONALLY.

IN 1931, HE TOOK A BIG TRIP TO EUROPE, WHERE HE RECEIVED A WARM WELCOME.

IN ENGLAND, HE MET WITH TEXTILE WORKERS AND ALSO THE KING AND QUEEN, WHOM HE HAD TEA WITH!

DID HE MANAGE TO CONVINCE THE BRITISH TO LEAVE INDIA?

NOT THEN... IN ENGLAND, THE MPS GOVERNED, AND THEY LOOKED DOWN ON GANDHI'S ACTIONS.

ONE OF THEM, **WINSTON CHURCHILL**, DIDN'T TRUST HIM.

A FAKIR...

HALF NAKED!

THE BRITISH REMAINED STRONGER AND DIDN'T WANT TO LET GO OF INDIA, THE "JEWEL IN THE CROWN OF THE BRITISH EMPIRE," WHICH GAVE THEM THEIR POWER!

BUT WWII WOULD CHANGE ALL THAT.

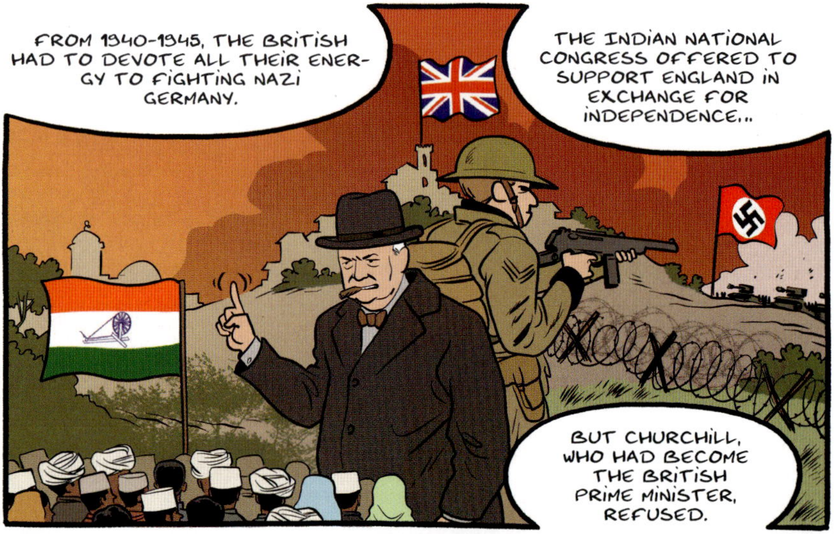

FROM 1940-1945, THE BRITISH HAD TO DEVOTE ALL THEIR ENERGY TO FIGHTING NAZI GERMANY.

THE INDIAN NATIONAL CONGRESS OFFERED TO SUPPORT ENGLAND IN EXCHANGE FOR INDEPENDENCE...

BUT CHURCHILL, WHO HAD BECOME THE BRITISH PRIME MINISTER, REFUSED.

THE BRITISH THREW HIM IN JAIL AGAIN, THIS TIME FOR TWO YEARS! HIS WIFE KASTURBA DIED IN PRISON.

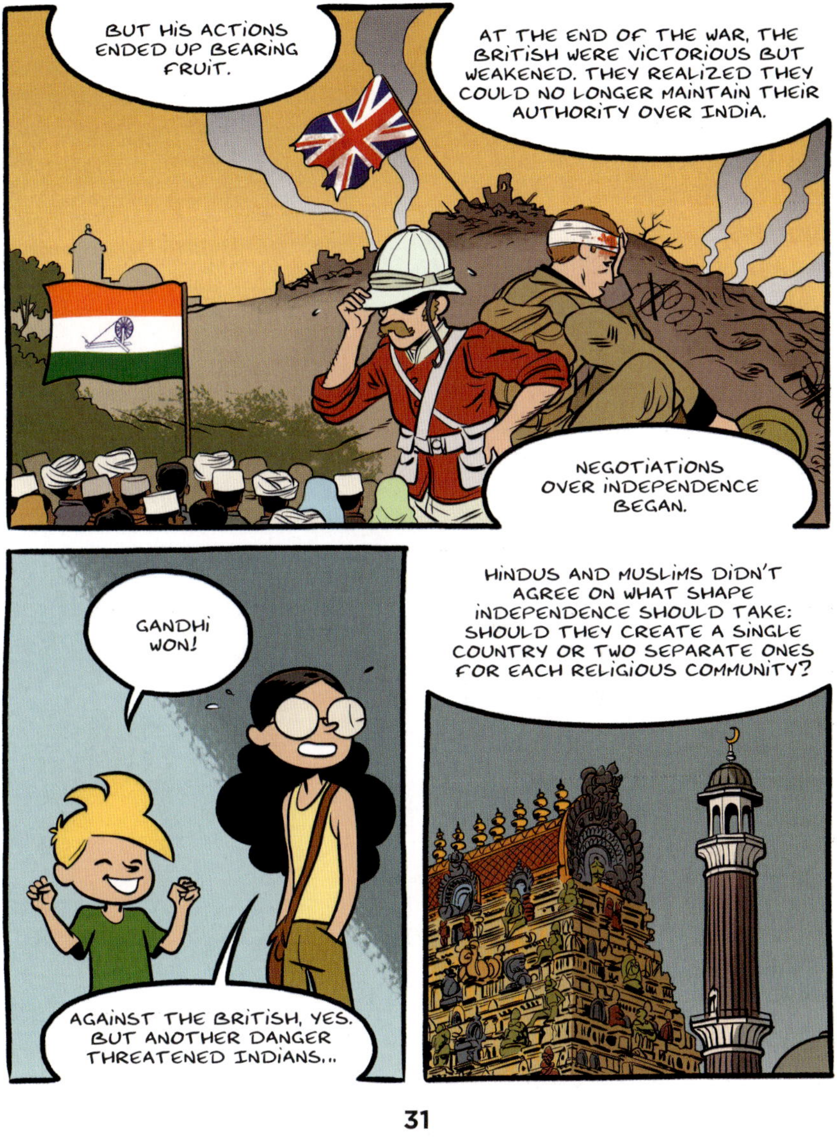

BUT HIS ACTIONS ENDED UP BEARING FRUIT.

AT THE END OF THE WAR, THE BRITISH WERE VICTORIOUS BUT WEAKENED. THEY REALIZED THEY COULD NO LONGER MAINTAIN THEIR AUTHORITY OVER INDIA.

NEGOTIATIONS OVER INDEPENDENCE BEGAN.

HINDUS AND MUSLIMS DIDN'T AGREE ON WHAT SHAPE INDEPENDENCE SHOULD TAKE: SHOULD THEY CREATE A SINGLE COUNTRY OR TWO SEPARATE ONES FOR EACH RELIGIOUS COMMUNITY?

GANDHI HAD TRIED TO RECONCILE THE TWO COMMUNITIES FOR YEARS. HE FELT THAT INDIANS SHOULD LIVE TOGETHER.

BUT THE INDIAN NATIONAL CONGRESS, WHICH NEHRU THEN LED, CONSISTED MOSTLY OF HINDUS...

AND THE MUSLIMS HAD THEIR OWN PARTY, THE **"MUSLIM LEAGUE,"** LED BY **MUHAMMAD ALI JINNAH.**

THIS CONFLICT BROUGHT ABOUT HUGE CLASHES.

THOUSANDS OF PEOPLE WERE KILLED WITHIN THE TWO COMMUNITIES.

FOR GANDHI, THIS WAS AN ENORMOUS FAILURE, NOT JUST THAT INDIANS WERE DIVIDED BUT ALSO THE INTENSE VIOLENCE.

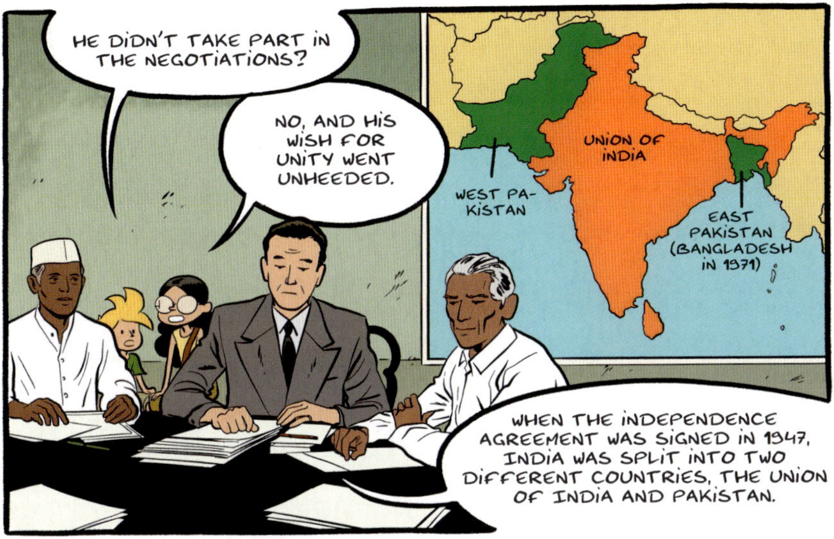

HE DIDN'T TAKE PART IN THE NEGOTIATIONS?

NO, AND HIS WISH FOR UNITY WENT UNHEEDED.

WEST PAKISTAN

UNION OF INDIA

EAST PAKISTAN (BANGLADESH IN 1971)

WHEN THE INDEPENDENCE AGREEMENT WAS SIGNED IN 1947, INDIA WAS SPLIT INTO TWO DIFFERENT COUNTRIES, THE UNION OF INDIA AND PAKISTAN.

YES, THOSE WERE THE AREAS WHERE THERE WERE THE MOST MUSLIMS. BUT 12 MILLION PEOPLE HAD TO MOVE TO GET TO THEIR NEW COUNTY AND THE VIOLENCE CONTINUED DURING THE CRISSCROSSING.

ON JANUARY 13, 1948, GANDHI WHO WAS HINDU, BEGAN A FAST TO STOP THE VIOLENCE AGAINST MUSLIMS, YET ANOTHER SYMBOL OF RECONCILIATION.

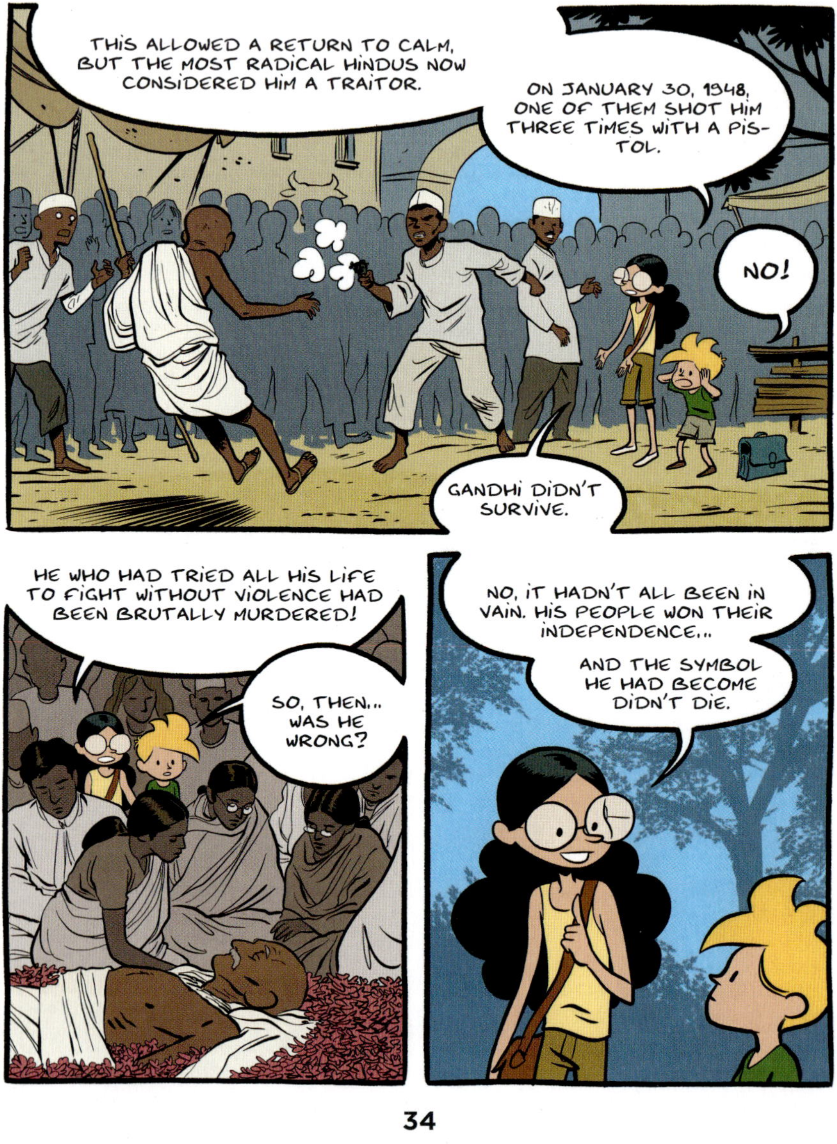

THIS ALLOWED A RETURN TO CALM, BUT THE MOST RADICAL HINDUS NOW CONSIDERED HIM A TRAITOR.
ON JANUARY 30, 1948, ONE OF THEM SHOT HIM THREE TIMES WITH A PIS-TOL.
NO!
GANDHI DIDN'T SURVIVE.

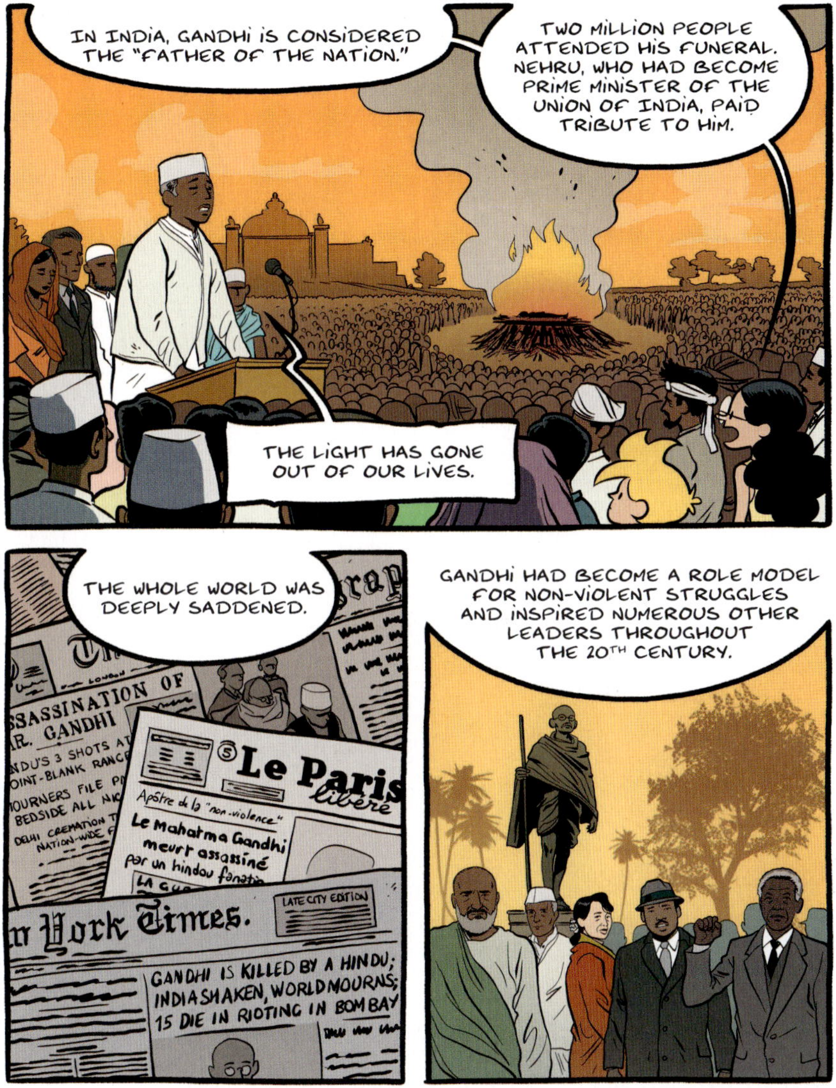

IN INDIA, GANDHI IS CONSIDERED THE "FATHER OF THE NATION."

TWO MILLION PEOPLE ATTENDED HIS FUNERAL. NEHRU, WHO HAD BECOME PRIME MINISTER OF THE UNION OF INDIA, PAID TRIBUTE TO HIM.

THE LIGHT HAS GONE OUT OF OUR LIVES.

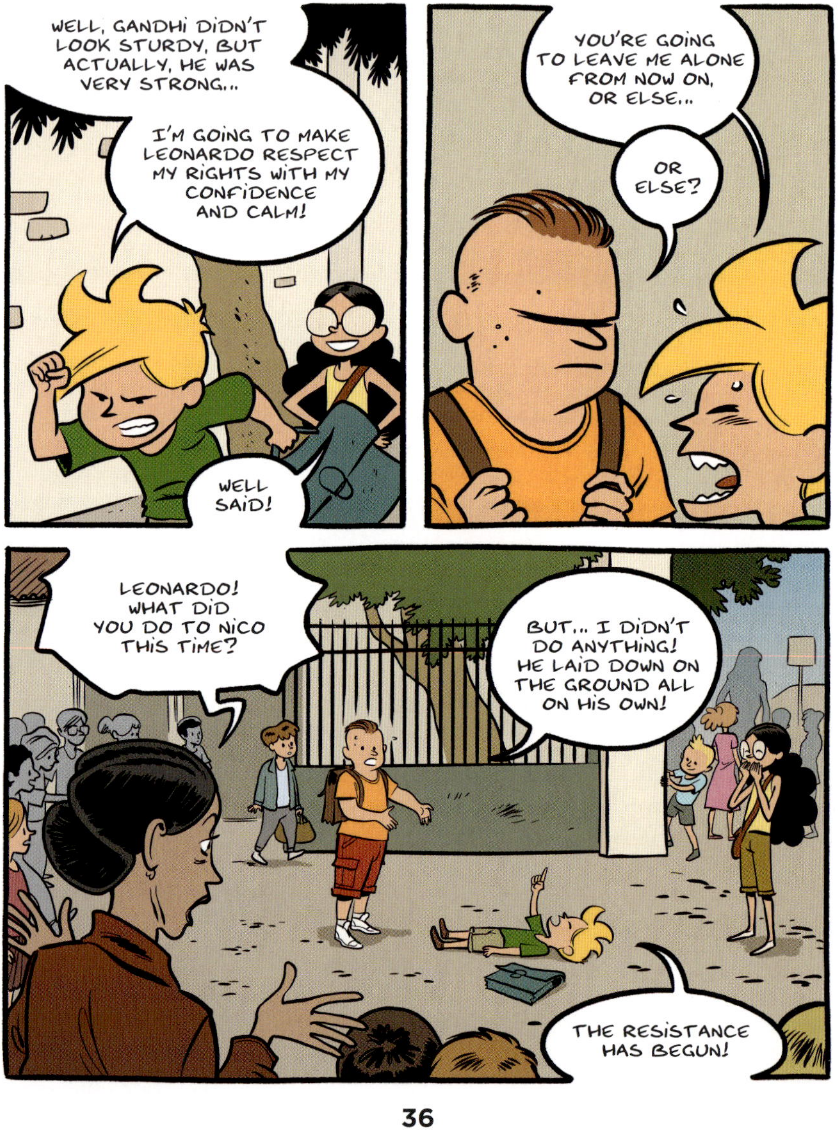

LEONARDO! WHAT DID YOU DO TO NICO THIS TIME?

BUT... I DIDN'T DO ANYTHING! HE LAID DOWN ON THE GROUND ALL ON HIS OWN!

THE RESISTANCE HAS BEGUN!

And there's more...

Some People Who Made History

Kasturbai "Kasturba" Mohandas
(1869-1944)

Married to Gandhi at age 13. They had four children together. She joined her husband in South Africa in 1896. It was sometimes hard for her to accept his beliefs (living a communal life, renouncing all property and sex...) but she supported everything he did, which earned her the nickname of "Ma" ("Mother") among Indians. Arrested in 1944, she died of bronchitis in jail.

Jawaharlal Nehru
(1889-1964)

Son of Motilal Nehru. An Indian independence activist, he met Gandhi in 1916 and supported his fight, which meant he was jailed many times. Elected president of the Indian National Congress in 1929, he negotiated with the British for India's independence, which was achieved in 1947. But he was unable to avoid India's being split into two countries. Nehru led the Union of India until his death in 1964. His daughter, **Indira Gandhi**, and his grandson, **Ravij Gandhi**, also led the country.

Annie Besant
(1847-1933)

Committed to defending women and workers, she was interested in theosophy (which brings together philosophy and religion) and met Gandhi in London during his studies there. She met him again in India, where she campaigned for independence, having herself been elected president of the Indian National Congress in 1917. Annie accepted Gandhi's symbolic role, but felt his strategy of protests—such as the one that caused the massacre at Amritsar—was dangerous.

Muhammad Ali Jinnah
(1876-1948)

Muslim Indian independence activist Jinnah originally supported unity between Hindus and Muslims, brokering an agreement between them (the Lucknow Pact in 1916). But he opposed Gandhi's strategy and left the Indian National Congress in 1920 to devote himself to his other party, the Muslim League, which he led. Upon India's independence in 1947, he negotiated the creation of Pakistan against Gandhi's advice, and became its Governor-General.

The Indian Subcontinent

The colonial British Empire united two very different populations and regions. Gandhi wanted to free them but above all, he wanted to unite them, too. He was hampered by difficulties he could not overcome.

Ever since the Middle Ages, the term "Indies," was used by Europeans to designate the vast region of South Asia, an area much larger than today's India. The Indian Subcontinent had been colonized by several European nations (France, Portugal...) but **it was the British who made the largest conquest**. The region was first run by a commercial firm, the East India Company, and then starting in 1858, directly by the British king or queen: this ownership thus became the "**British Raj**" or "Indian Empire."

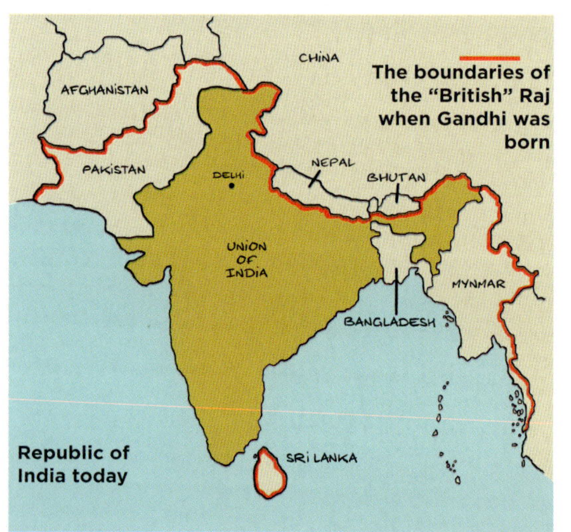

A British "viceroy" ran part of the region in person, directly. There were also "princely states," which retained an Indian ruler under British authority. Gandhi's father, Karamchand, was the Prime Minister of the "rana" (ruler) of Porbandar, like his father before him. Thus, power could be shared (although unequally) between British and Indians.

In 1885, the British and educated Indians founded the "Indian National Congress" to let the local population participate in the government. This organization campaigned for independence when Gandhi joined it.

Hindus praying to Ganesh.

The inhabitants of the Indies were "Indians," a term referring to different populations at that time. **"Hindus" are a religious community** that believes in multiple gods, such as Shiva, Ganesh, and Vishnu. There are other religious communities, particularly Muslims, **Indians who converted to Islam** starting in the 8th century. So there are Hindu Indians and Muslim Indians (and also Sikh, Christian, and Buddhist Indians...). **Tensions between the two communities had existed since the 14th century** (Muslim conquests...) but grew in the 20th century: if the country gained its independence, each community wondered whether it would be respected as equal to the other.

Muslims praying to their one god.

Dividing the Indies into two countries (Union of India and Pakistan) in 1947 didn't separate the two populations completely and there was still violence between them. But there were also clashes with the other communities: **Indira Gandhi**, leader of the Union of India, was assassinated in 1984 by her own Sikh bodyguards.

Non-violence

Gandhi invented the term "non-violence" in 1920. He was inspired by a number of movements and figures, and he led the way for other similar struggles in the 20th century.

Gandhi was first interested in several types of religious messages, starting during his stay in London. In Indian traditions (Hinduism, Jainism), **ahimsa is an important principle that involves not harming another life.** This principle, in particular, led Gandhi to be a vegetarian. In the Christian religion, Christ teaches to "turn the other cheek," when one has been hit, rather than hitting back. In the Koran, the prophet Mohammed advocates "patience" and "forgiveness."

Leo Tolstoy at his desk in 1908.

Writers also guided and helped Gandhi. **Leo Tolstoy,** the Russian author of *War and Peace*, **wrote *A Letter to a Hindu* in 1908,** in which he explained to an Indian separatist that violence could not free his country. Gandhi, greatly influenced by these words, exchanged many letters with Tolstoy and named one of his "ashrams" (retreats in secluded locations) "Tolstoy Farm."

Gandhi served as a model for other leaders. In the United States, **starting in the 1950s, Reverend Martin Luther King Jr. fought against the discrimination that Blacks suffered in some states.** He used the same methods as Gandhi (boycotts, marches) and succeeded in having the rights of Blacks recognized. He was assassinated in 1968, twenty years after Gandhi.

Martin Luther King Jr. posing below a portrait of Gandhi.

In South Africa, where Gandhi began his career, **Nelson Mandela opposed the system of apartheid that separated white and Black people** by organizing acts of civil disobedience, beginning in 1948. He was imprisoned for 27 years. After his release, he was elected president of South Africa and worked hard to reconcile the two populations.

In Myanmar, **Aung San Suu Kyi, an opponent of the military dictatorship, was inspired by Gandhi to protest against it in 1988.** She founded the National League for Democracy and endorsed a huge general strike. Jailed numerous times over more than twenty years, she became a symbol of non-violent resistance. Her party ended up winning the election and leading the country before a new military coup ousted and jailed her.

Timeline

October 2, 1869
Birth of Mohandas Gandhi in Porbandar (India).

1888
Gandhi leaves for London to study law

1919
Amritsar Massacre: The army fires upon a peaceful Indian protest.

1930
At the "Salt March," Gandhi symbolically lays claim to a handful of salt.

1931
Gandhi's major trip to Europe: he is very popular but doesn't win independence for India.

1942
In the midst of WWII, Gandhi launches the "Quit India movement" against the British.

1893

Gandhi personally faces racism in South Africa.

1906

Gandhi sets out the non-violent principle of "satyagraha" ("the force of truth").

1913

Large non-violent protest by Indians in South Africa.

1915

Gandhi returns to India to gain "swaraj" ("independence").

August 15, 1947

Independence of India and Pakistan.

January 30, 1948

Gandhi assassinated by a Hindu extremist In New Delhi (India).

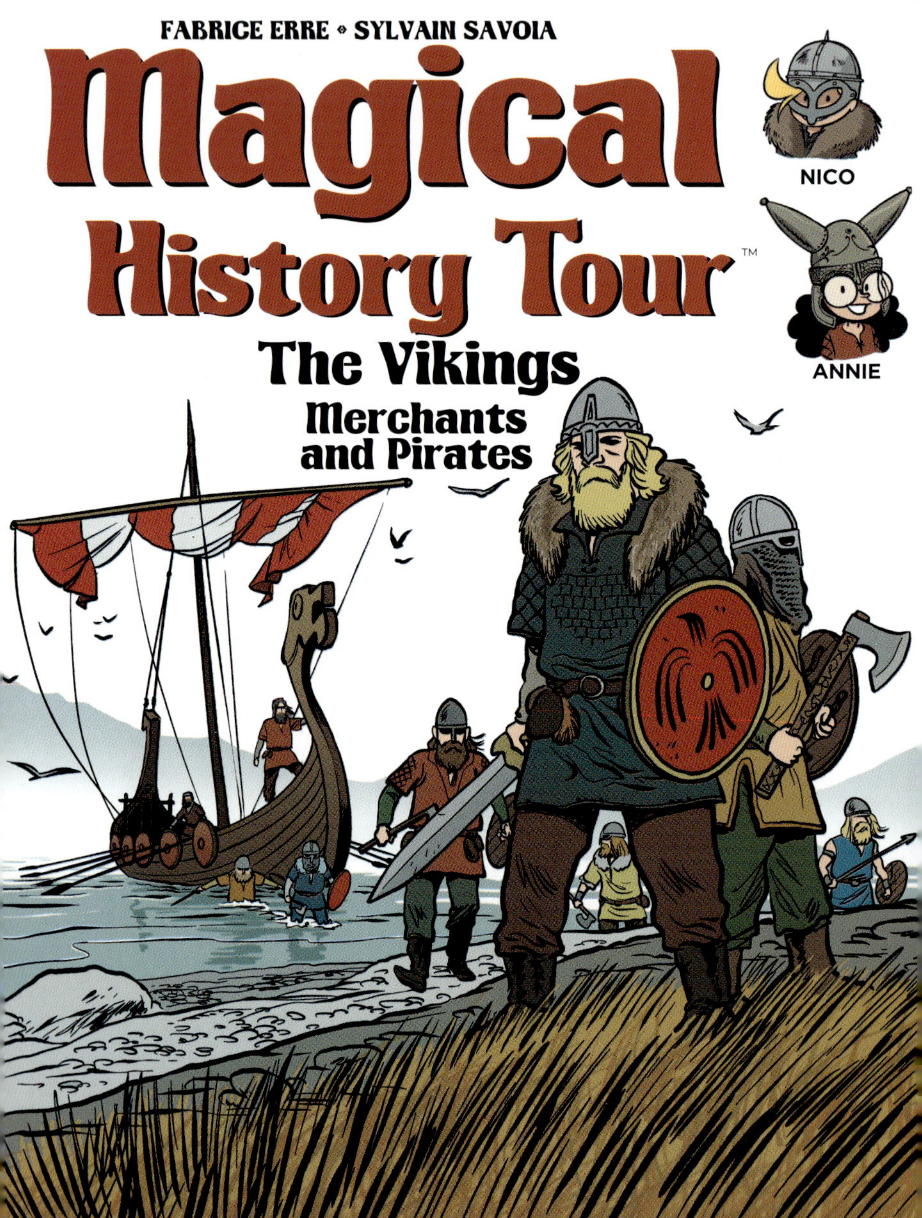
FABRICE ERRE • SYLVAIN SAVOIA
Magical History Tour™
The Vikings
Merchants and Pirates
NICO
ANNIE

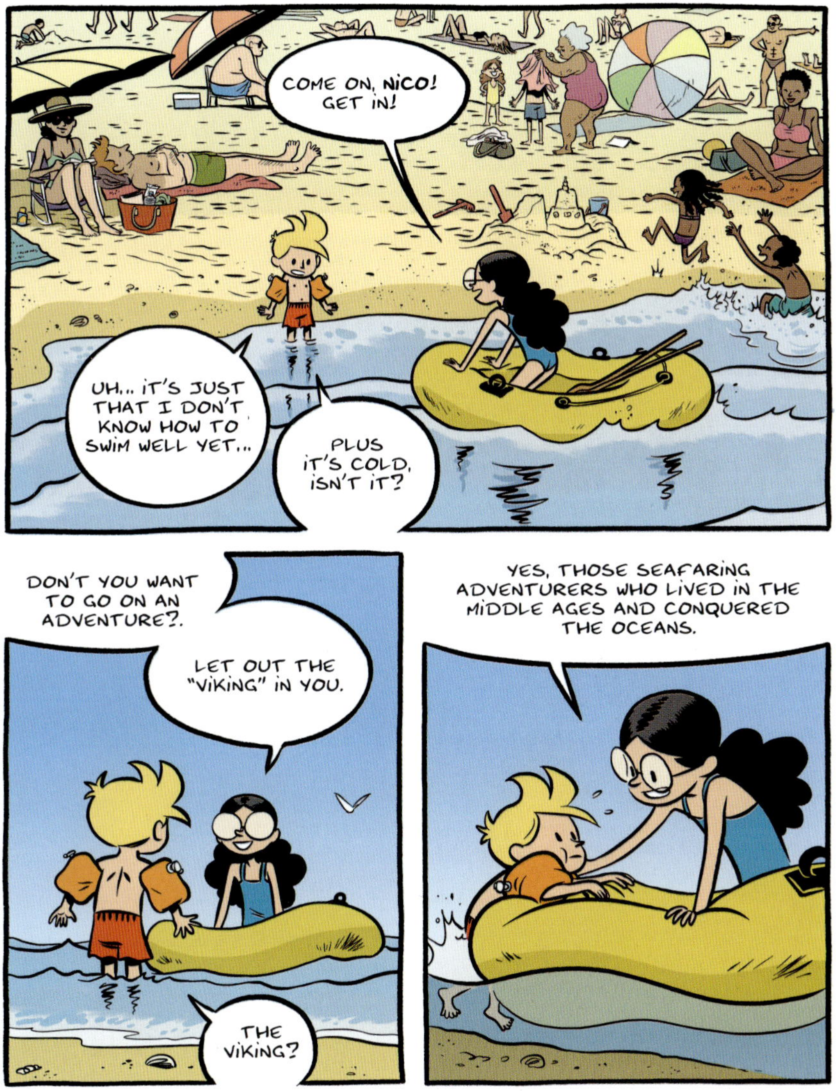

COME ON, NICO! GET IN!

UH... IT'S JUST THAT I DON'T KNOW HOW TO SWIM WELL YET...

PLUS IT'S COLD, ISN'T IT?

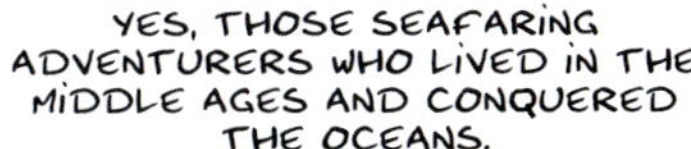

THESE "MEN OF THE NORTH," ALSO CALLED "NORMANS," CAME FROM SCANDINAVIA, A VAST REGION IN THE NORTH OF EUROPE.

IN THEIR LANGUAGE, "OLD NORSE," THE WORD "VIKING" MAY MEAN "BAY" OR "CREEK."

THREE GROUPS OF PEOPLE LIVED THERE. SOME OF THEM TOOK TO THE SEA FOR CONQUEST. THEY WERE CALLED "VIKINGS."

NORTH SEA

NORWEIGANS

SWEDISH

BALTIC SEA

DANISH

THEY FIRST GATHERED IN SMALL GROUPS ON A FEW SHIPS WITH A CHIEFTAIN FOR A LEADER. THEY SAILED AWAY TO GET RICH.

SO ALL THE "NORMANS" DIDN'T BECOME "VIKINGS"?

NO, JUST THE MOST ADVENTUROUS. BUT THERE WERE STILL A LOT OF THEM.

THEY WERE KIND OF SCARY, RIGHT?

OH, YES! THEY TERRORIZED EUROPE BETWEEN THE 8TH AND 11TH CENTURIES!

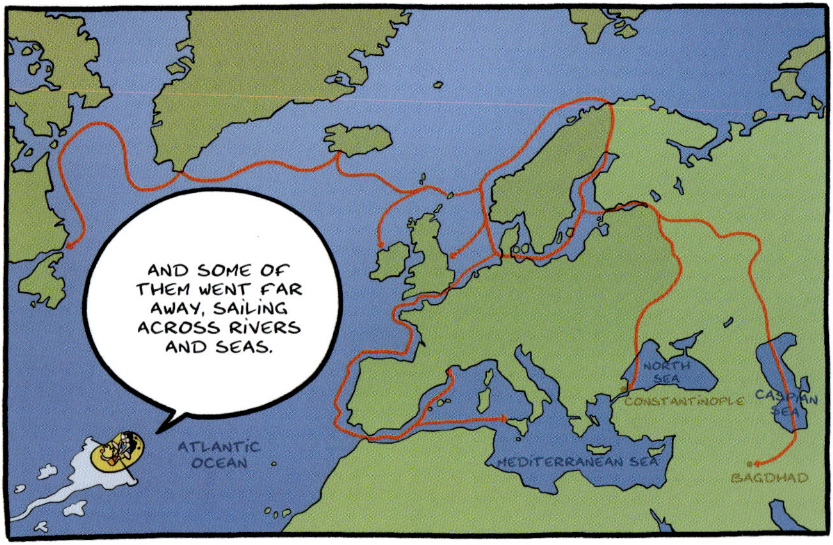

AND SOME OF THEM WENT FAR AWAY, SAILING ACROSS RIVERS AND SEAS.

NORTH SEA

CONSTANTINOPLE

CASPIAN SEA

ATLANTIC OCEAN

MEDITERRANEAN SEA

BAGDHAD

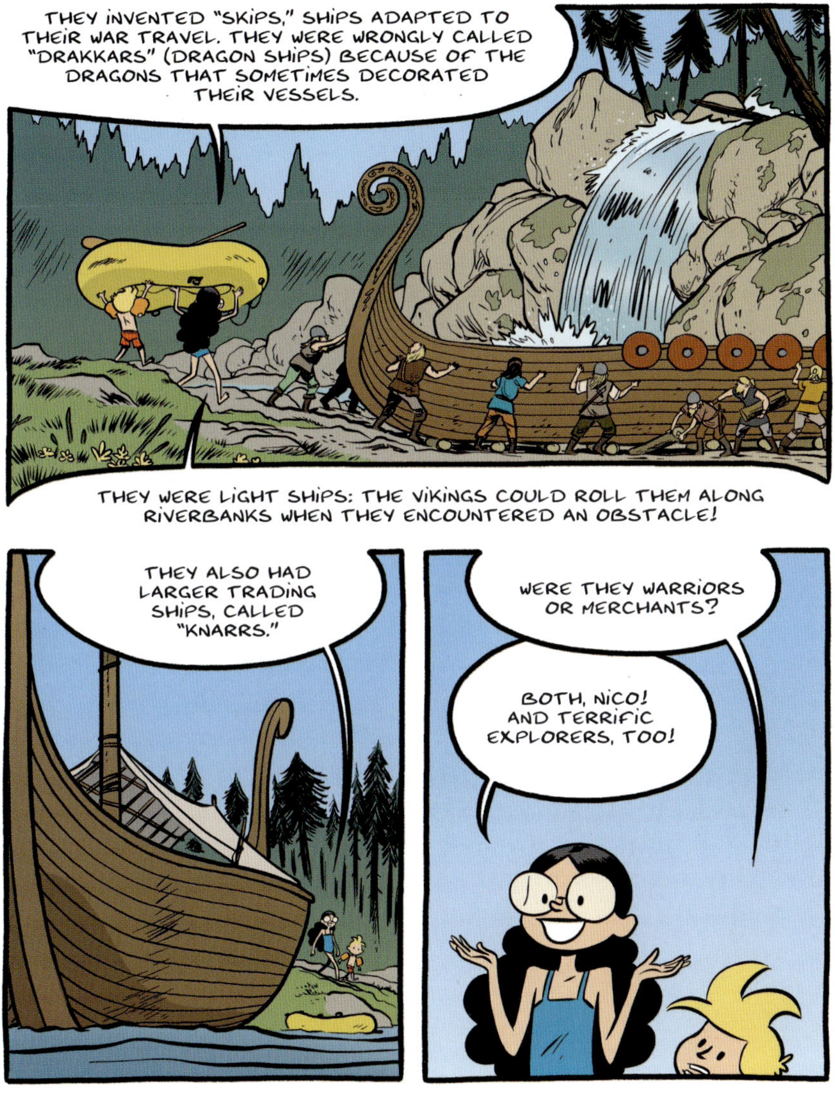

THEY INVENTED "SKIPS," SHIPS ADAPTED TO THEIR WAR TRAVEL. THEY WERE WRONGLY CALLED "DRAKKARS" (DRAGON SHIPS) BECAUSE OF THE DRAGONS THAT SOMETIMES DECORATED THEIR VESSELS.

THEY WERE LIGHT SHIPS: THE VIKINGS COULD ROLL THEM ALONG RIVERBANKS WHEN THEY ENCOUNTERED AN OBSTACLE!

THEY STARTED TO TRAVEL THE WORLD TO TRADE...
ARTISANS, HUNTERS, FARMERS... THEY HAD LOTS OF THINGS TO SELL.

WHAT'S THAT?
WALRUS IVORY. IT'S AS VALUABLE AS IVORY FROM ELE-PHANTS.

"SILENT TRADE" CONSISTED OF LEAVING MERCHANDISE IN A PLACE AND COMING BACK LATER TO SEE IF SOMEONE MADE A TRADE.
NO ONE STOLE IT?

YOU'D WANT TO STEAL FROM THIS GUY?
GULP! NO!

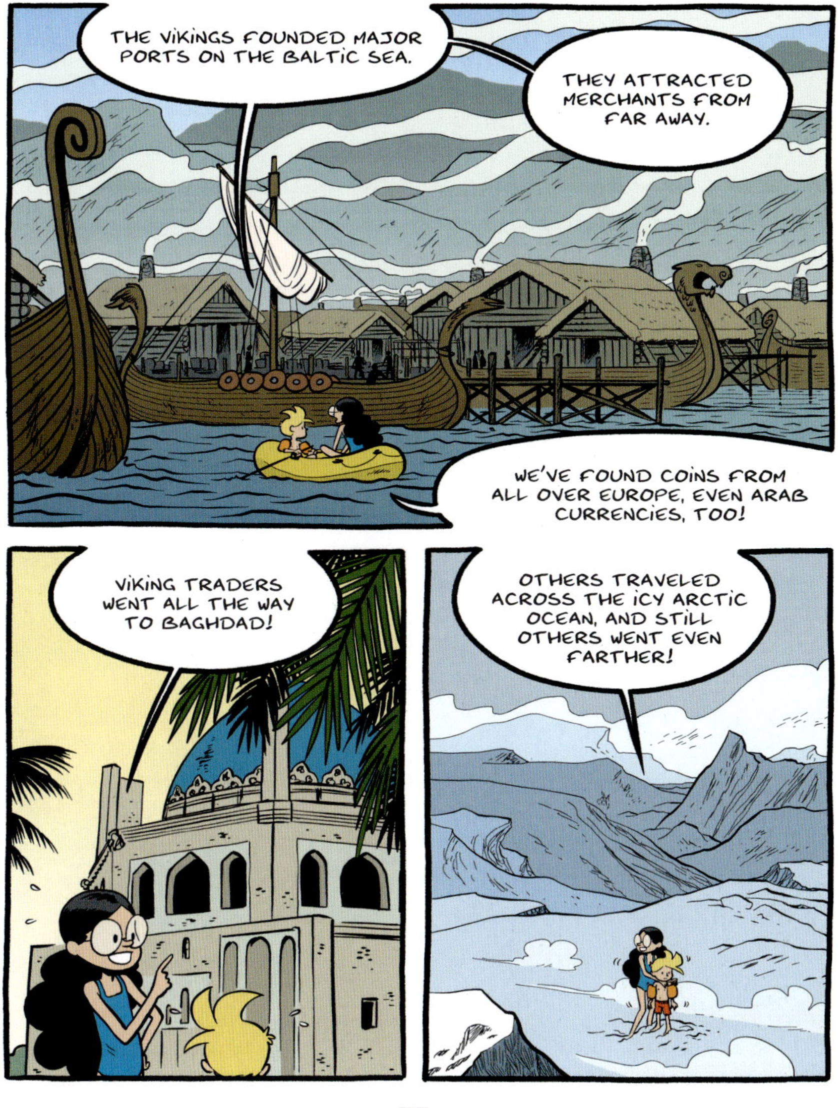

THE VIKINGS FOUNDED MAJOR PORTS ON THE BALTIC SEA.
THEY ATTRACTED MERCHANTS FROM FAR AWAY.
WE'VE FOUND COINS FROM ALL OVER EUROPE, EVEN ARAB CURRENCIES, TOO!

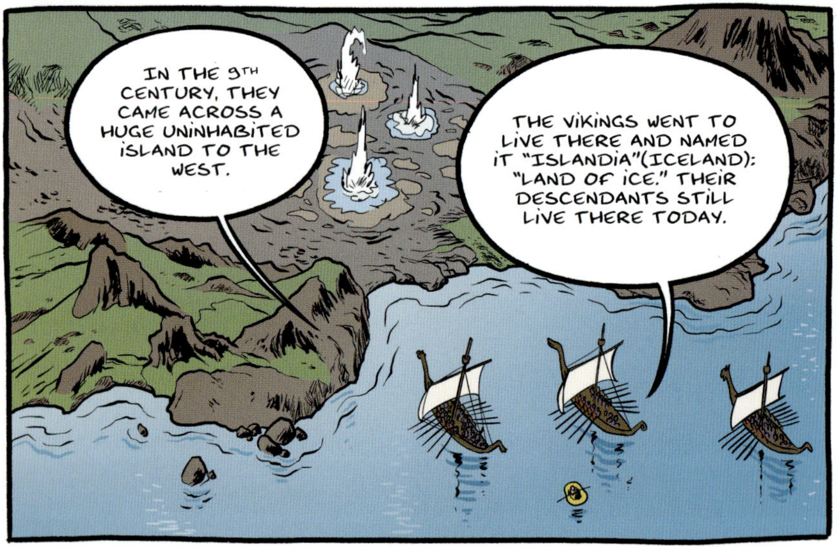

IN THE 9TH CENTURY, THEY CAME ACROSS A HUGE UNINHABITED ISLAND TO THE WEST.

THE VIKINGS WENT TO LIVE THERE AND NAMED IT "ISLANDIA"(ICELAND): "LAND OF ICE." THEIR DESCENDANTS STILL LIVE THERE TODAY.

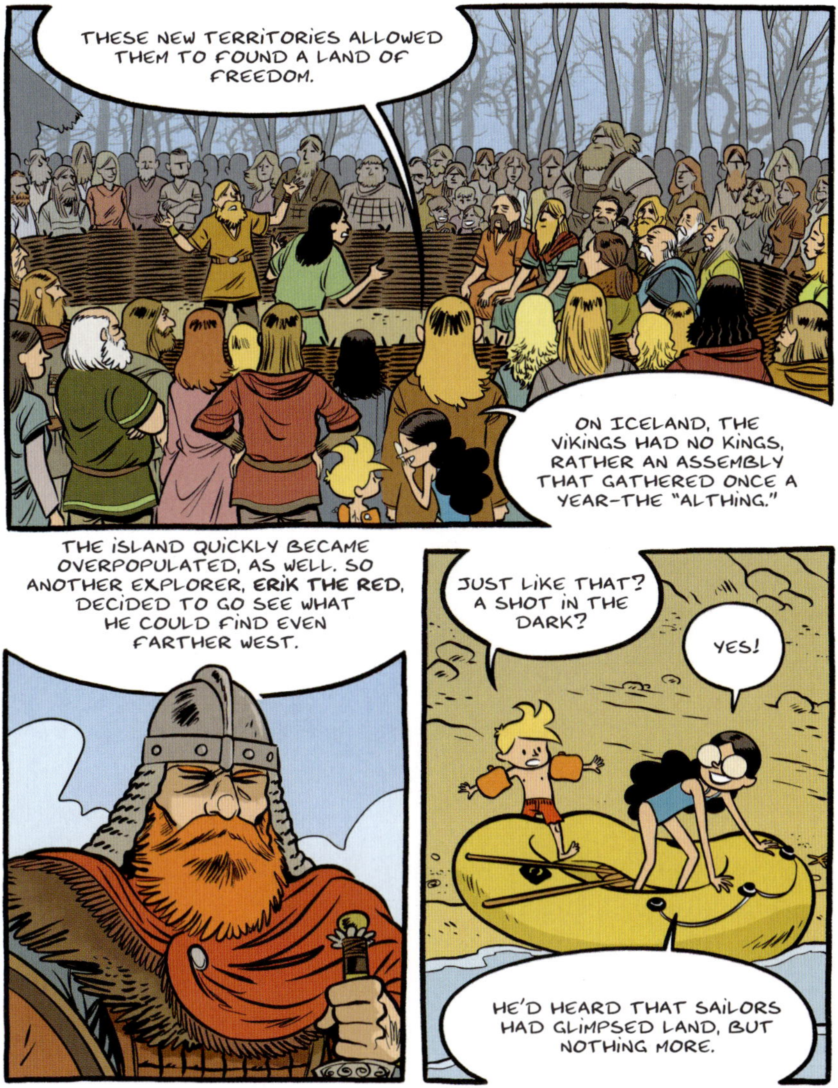

THESE NEW TERRITORIES ALLOWED THEM TO FOUND A LAND OF FREEDOM.

ON ICELAND, THE VIKINGS HAD NO KINGS, RATHER AN ASSEMBLY THAT GATHERED ONCE A YEAR—THE "ALTHING."

THE ISLAND QUICKLY BECAME OVERPOPULATED, AS WELL. SO ANOTHER EXPLORER, **ERIK THE RED**, DECIDED TO GO SEE WHAT HE COULD FIND EVEN FARTHER WEST.

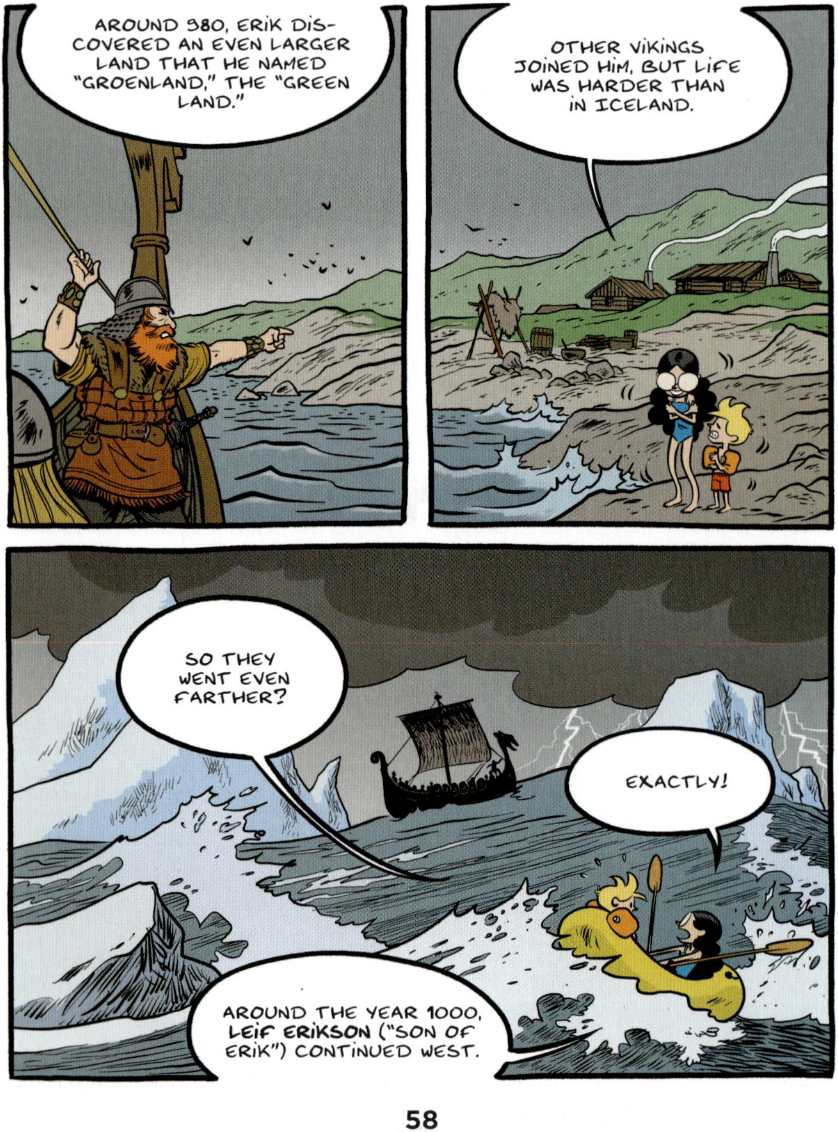

SO THEY WENT EVEN FARTHER?

EXACTLY!

AROUND THE YEAR 1000, **LEIF ERIKSON** ("SON OF ERIK") CONTINUED WEST.

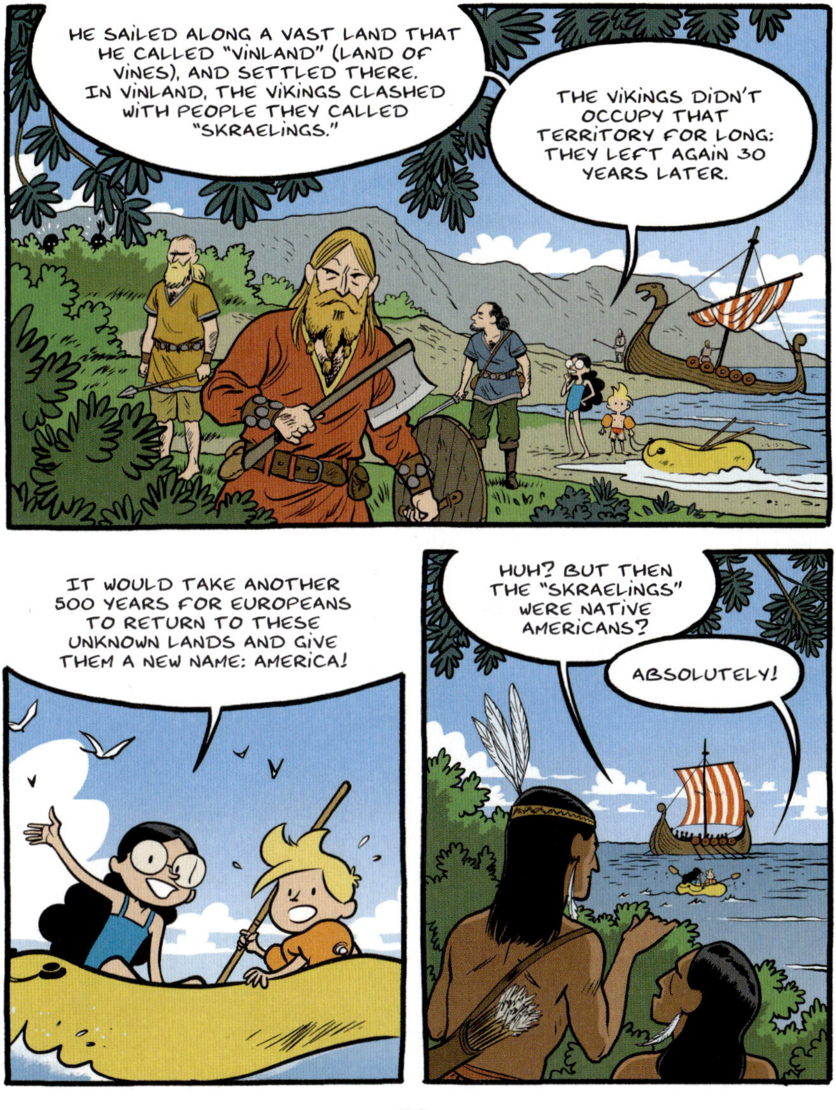

HE SAILED ALONG A VAST LAND THAT HE CALLED "VINLAND" (LAND OF VINES), AND SETTLED THERE. IN VINLAND, THE VIKINGS CLASHED WITH PEOPLE THEY CALLED "SKRAELINGS."

THE VIKINGS DIDN'T OCCUPY THAT TERRITORY FOR LONG: THEY LEFT AGAIN 30 YEARS LATER.

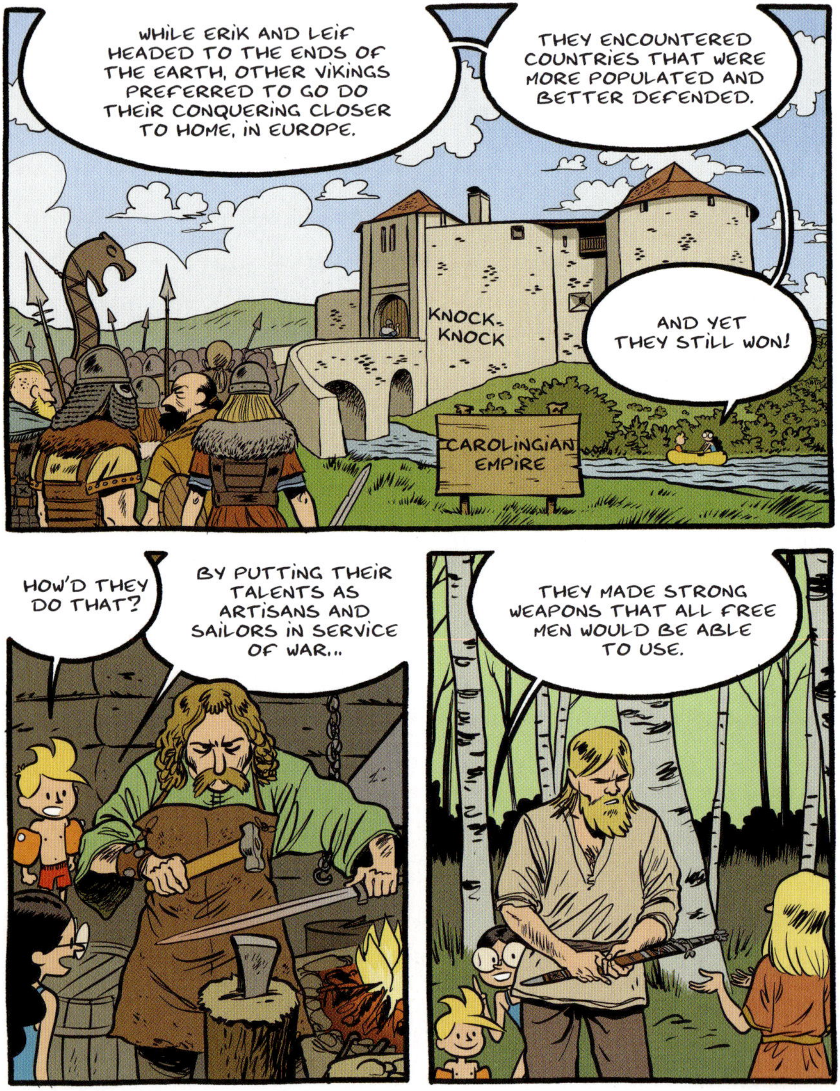

WHILE ERIK AND LEIF HEADED TO THE ENDS OF THE EARTH, OTHER VIKINGS PREFERRED TO GO DO THEIR CONQUERING CLOSER TO HOME, IN EUROPE.

THEY ENCOUNTERED COUNTRIES THAT WERE MORE POPULATED AND BETTER DEFENDED.

KNOCK-KNOCK

AND YET THEY STILL WON!

CAROLINGIAN EMPIRE

SWORDS, JAVELINS, AXES... THE RICH HAD BEAUTIFUL WEAPONS AS A SYMBOL OF THEIR POWER.

AND THE VIKINGS' "SKIPS," WHICH WERE VERY LIGHT, COULD GO IN EITHER DIRECTION...

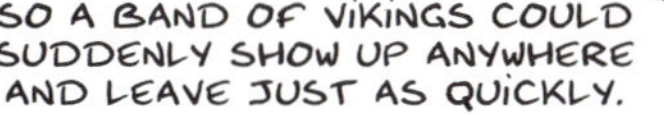
SO A BAND OF VIKINGS COULD SUDDENLY SHOW UP ANYWHERE AND LEAVE JUST AS QUICKLY.

PLUS THE VIKINGS HAD ANOTHER ADVANTAGE: THEY WEREN'T AFRAID OF DYING... JUST THE OPPOSITE!
OH, YEAH?

THEIR RELIGIOUS BELIEFS WERE WARLIKE.
THE KING OF THEIR GODS, **ODIN**, HAD A MAGIC SPEAR AND HIS SON, **THOR**, HAD A HAMMER.
WHEN A VIKING DIED FIGHTING, HE WAS CARRIED AWAY BY **THE VALKYRIES**, WARRIOR DEITIES.
THEY WOULD LEAD THEM TO VALHALLA, A GREAT HALL IN ASGARD RULED BY ODIN, WHERE THEY WOULD FIGHT AND FEAST UNTIL THE END OF TIME.
THE VIKINGS FEARED A "STRAW DEATH," THAT IS, DYING IN THEIR BEDS, A LOT MORE: THEIR SOULS WOULD THEN WANDER IN A PLACE OF DARKNESS FOR ETERNITY.
VALHALLA
HEL

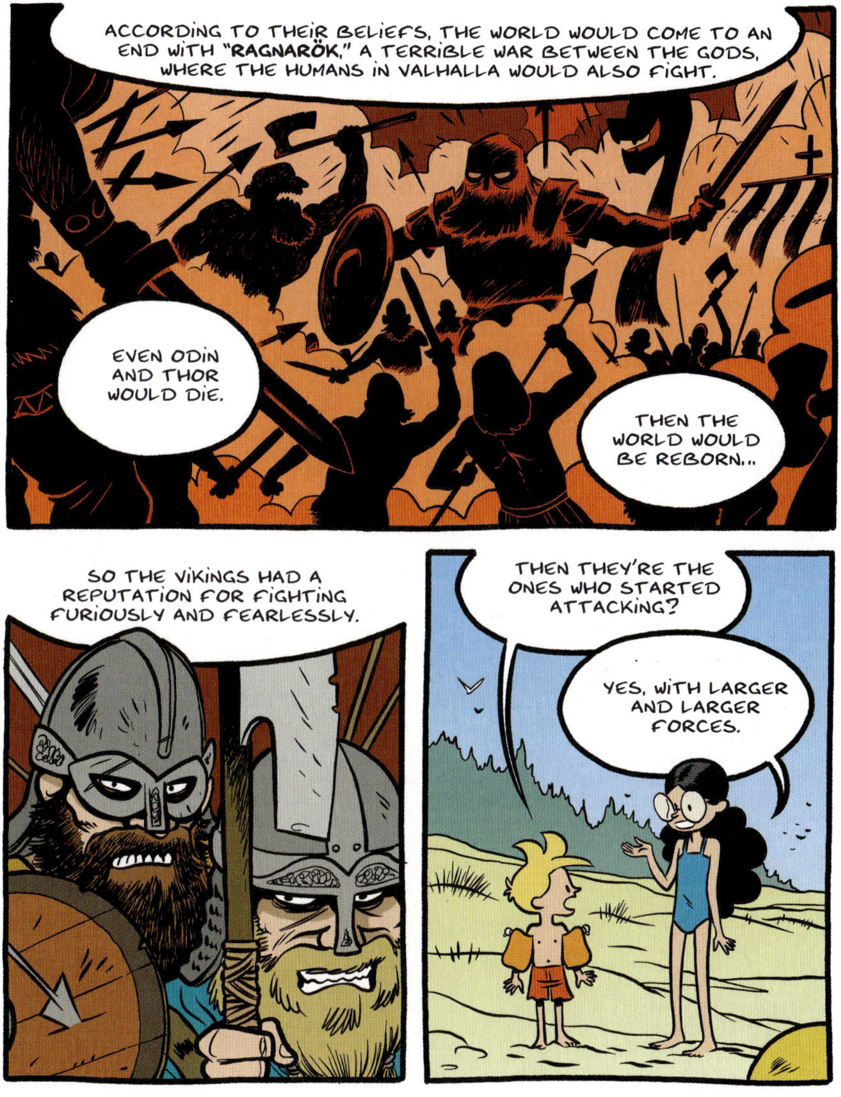

ACCORDING TO THEIR BELIEFS, THE WORLD WOULD COME TO AN END WITH "**RAGNARÖK**," A TERRIBLE WAR BETWEEN THE GODS, WHERE THE HUMANS IN VALHALLA WOULD ALSO FIGHT.

EVEN ODIN AND THOR WOULD DIE.

THEN THE WORLD WOULD BE REBORN...

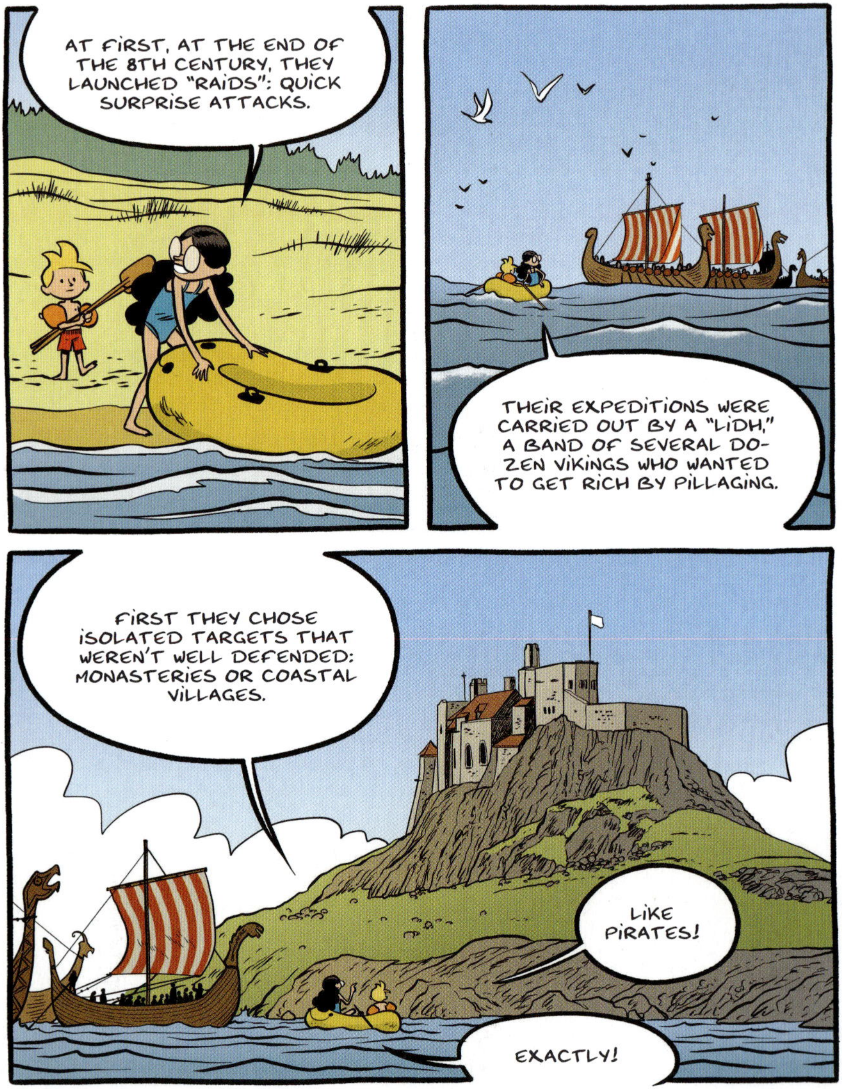

FIRST THEY CHOSE ISOLATED TARGETS THAT WEREN'T WELL DEFENDED: MONASTERIES OR COASTAL VILLAGES.

LIKE PIRATES!

EXACTLY!

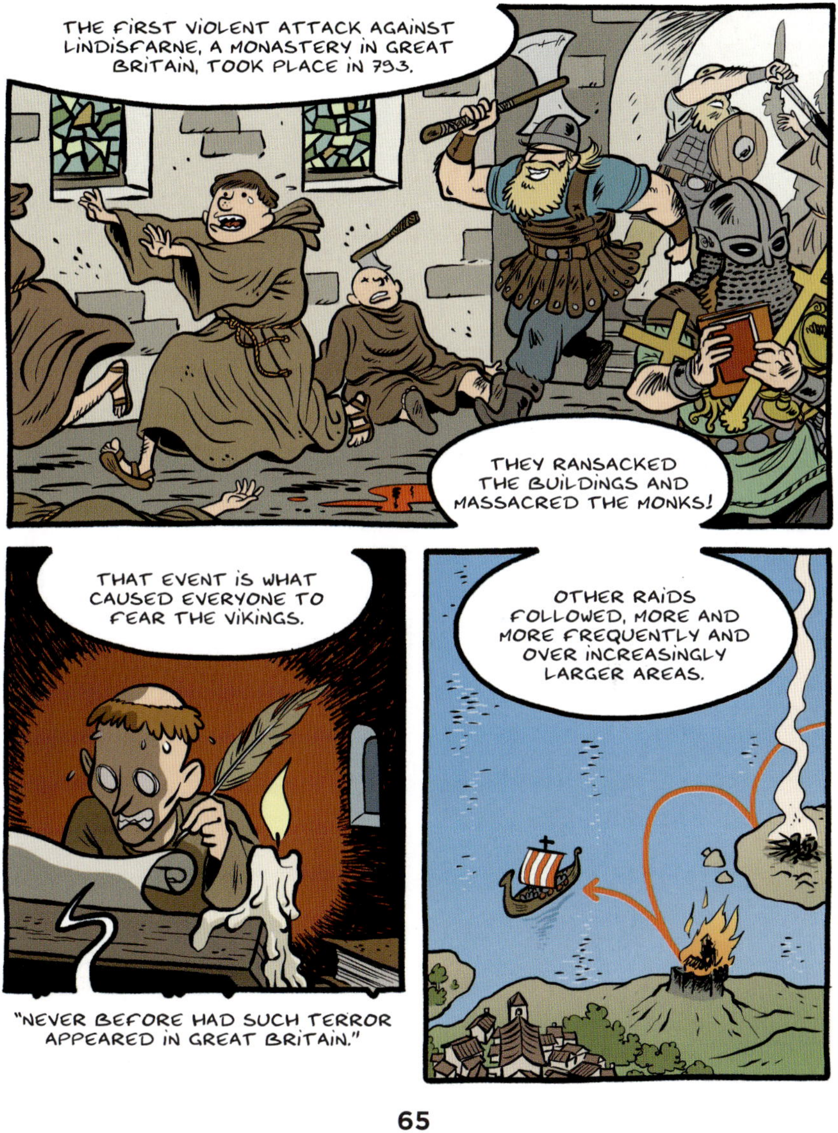

THE FIRST VIOLENT ATTACK AGAINST LINDISFARNE, A MONASTERY IN GREAT BRITAIN, TOOK PLACE IN 793.

THEY RANSACKED THE BUILDINGS AND MASSACRED THE MONKS!

"NEVER BEFORE HAD SUCH TERROR APPEARED IN GREAT BRITAIN."

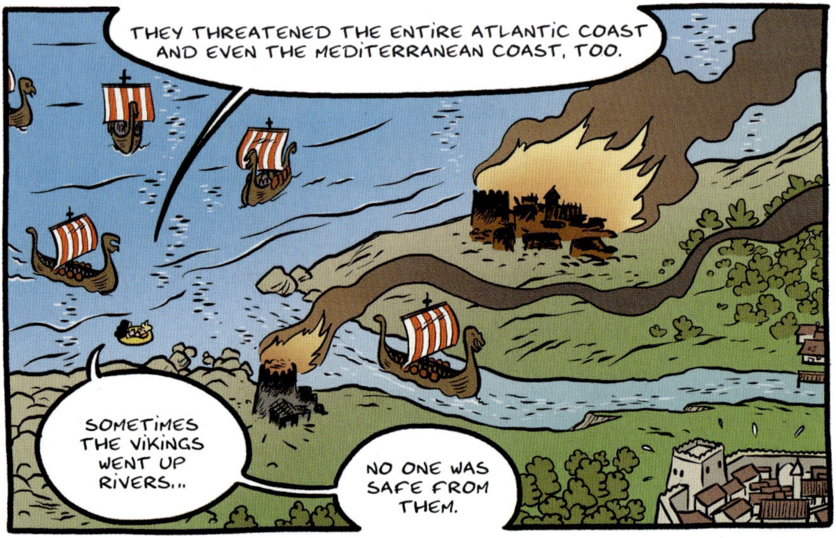

THEY THREATENED THE ENTIRE ATLANTIC COAST AND EVEN THE MEDITERRANEAN COAST, TOO.

SOMETIMES THE VIKINGS WENT UP RIVERS...

NO ONE WAS SAFE FROM THEM.

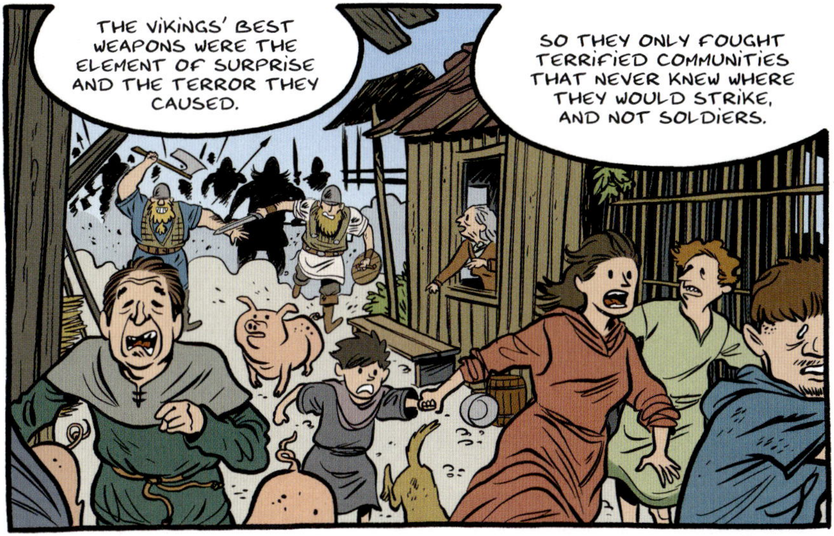

THE VIKINGS' BEST WEAPONS WERE THE ELEMENT OF SURPRISE AND THE TERROR THEY CAUSED.

SO THEY ONLY FOUGHT TERRIFIED COMMUNITIES THAT NEVER KNEW WHERE THEY WOULD STRIKE, AND NOT SOLDIERS.

THE ATTACKS BECAME EVEN MORE FREQUENT AND STRONGER.

FROM 865 TO 910, THE "GREAT VIKING ARMY" WREAKED HAVOC!

IN 885, 700 SHIPS LED BY **SIEGFRIED** WENT UP THE SEINE, ALL THE WAY TO PARIS. LED BY **COUNT ODO**, THE BATTLE TO DEFEND THE CITY LASTED FOR OVER A YEAR.

THE SURROUNDING COUNTRYSIDE WAS DEVASTATED DURING THIS TIME.

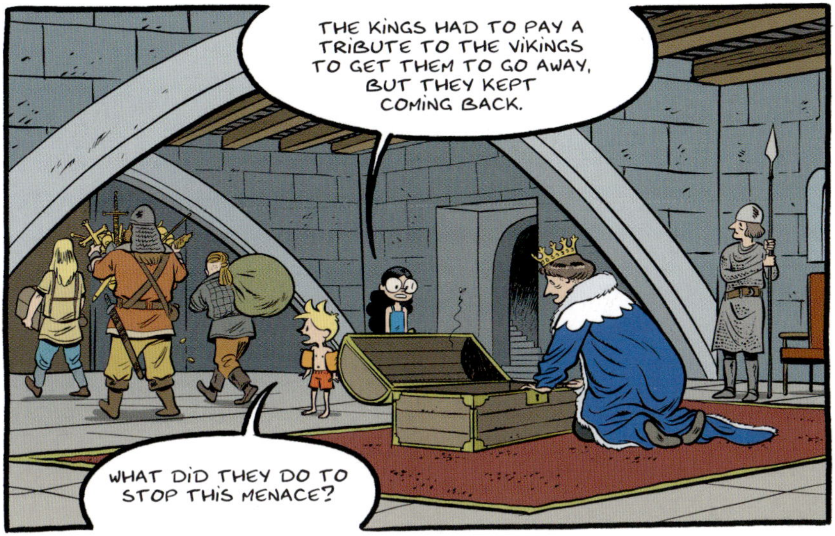

THE KINGS HAD TO PAY A TRIBUTE TO THE VIKINGS TO GET THEM TO GO AWAY, BUT THEY KEPT COMING BACK.

WHAT DID THEY DO TO STOP THIS MENACE?

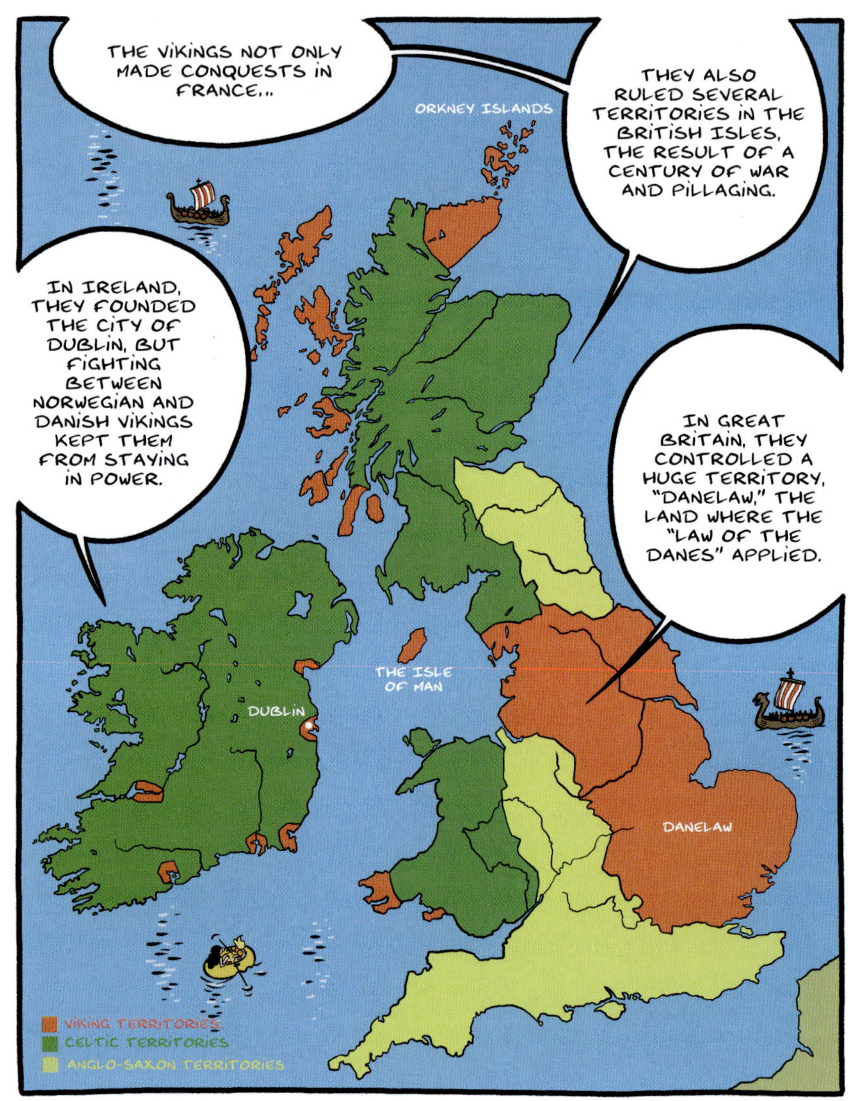
THE VIKINGS NOT ONLY MADE CONQUESTS IN FRANCE...
THEY ALSO RULED SEVERAL TERRITORIES IN THE BRITISH ISLES, THE RESULT OF A CENTURY OF WAR AND PILLAGING.
IN IRELAND, THEY FOUNDED THE CITY OF DUBLIN, BUT FIGHTING BETWEEN NORWEGIAN AND DANISH VIKINGS KEPT THEM FROM STAYING IN POWER.
IN GREAT BRITAIN, THEY CONTROLLED A HUGE TERRITORY, "DANELAW," THE LAND WHERE THE "LAW OF THE DANES" APPLIED.
ORKNEY ISLANDS
THE ISLE OF MAN
DUBLIN
DANELAW
VIKING TERRITORIES
CELTIC TERRITORIES
ANGLO-SAXON TERRITORIES

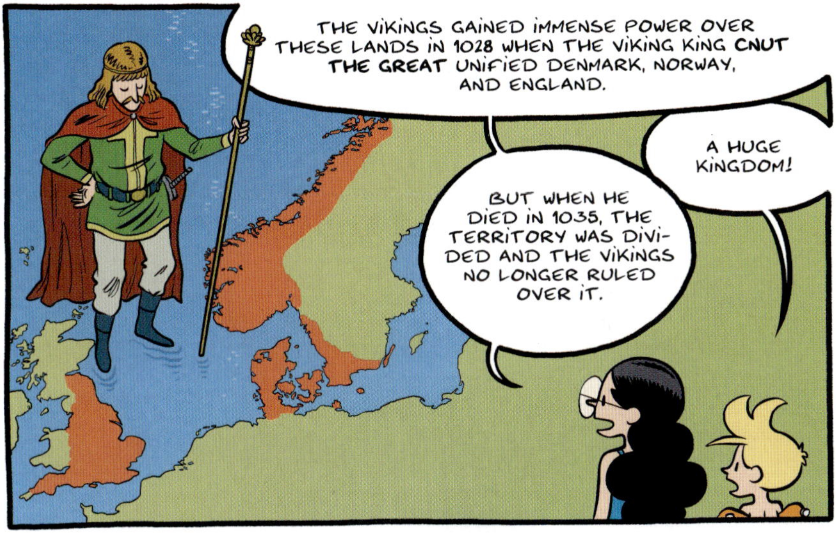

THE VIKINGS GAINED IMMENSE POWER OVER THESE LANDS IN 1028 WHEN THE VIKING KING **CNUT THE GREAT** UNIFIED DENMARK, NORWAY, AND ENGLAND.

A HUGE KINGDOM!

BUT WHEN HE DIED IN 1035, THE TERRITORY WAS DIVIDED AND THE VIKINGS NO LONGER RULED OVER IT.

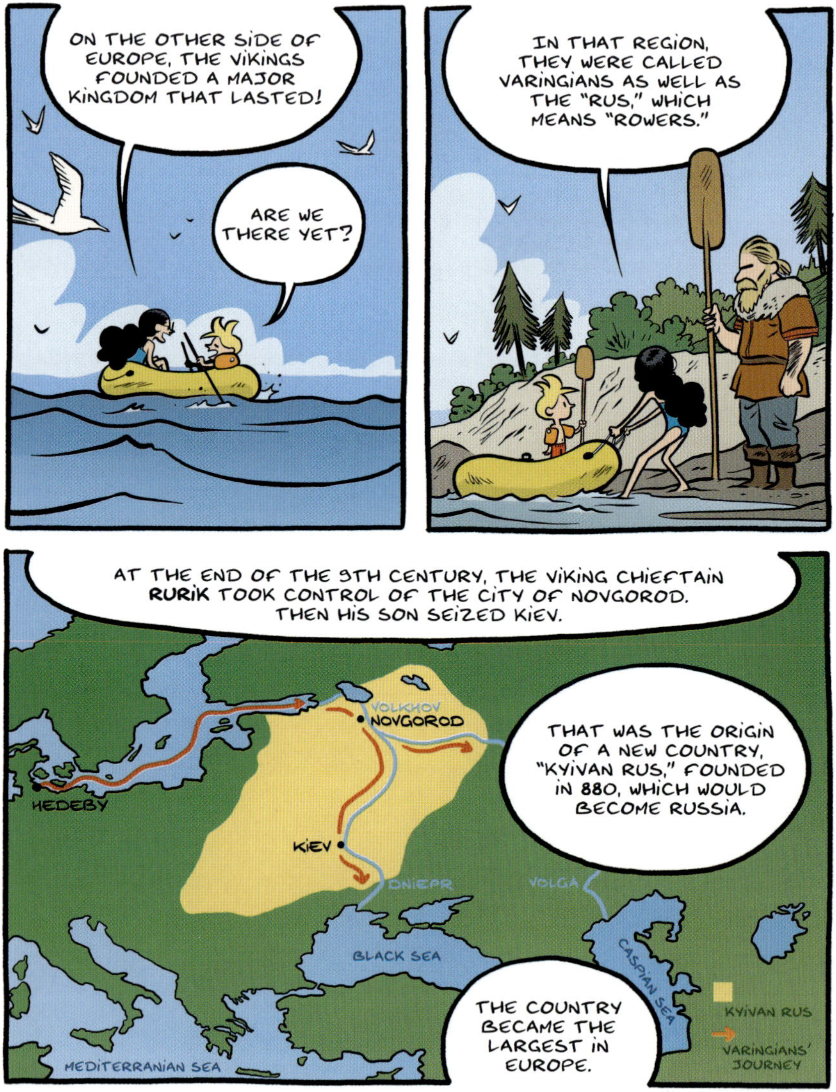

AT THE END OF THE 9TH CENTURY, THE VIKING CHIEFTAIN **RURIK** TOOK CONTROL OF THE CITY OF NOVGOROD. THEN HIS SON SEIZED KIEV.

VOLKHOV
NOVGOROD
HEDEBY
KIEV
DNIEPR
VOLGA
BLACK SEA
CASPIAN SEA
MEDITERRANIAN SEA
KYIVAN RUS
VARINGIANS' JOURNEY

THAT WAS THE ORIGIN OF A NEW COUNTRY, "KYIVAN RUS," FOUNDED IN 880, WHICH WOULD BECOME RUSSIA.

THE COUNTRY BECAME THE LARGEST IN EUROPE.

RURIK CONTROLLED ALL THE EASTERN EUROPEAN TRADE BETWEEN THE NORTHERN VIKINGS AND GREEK AND ARAB TRADERS.

THE VARINGIANS EVEN TRIED TO CONQUER CONSTANTINOPLE, THE CAPITAL OF THE POWERFUL BYZANTINE EMPIRE.

THE EMPEROR REPELLED THEM, BUT OFFERED THEM A DEAL: THEY COULD TRADE FREELY IN THE EMPIRE PROVIDED THEY DEFENDED IT INSTEAD OF ATTACKING IT.

SO THE VARINGIAN GUARD PERSONALLY PROTECTED THE EMPEROR FOR CENTURIES.

SINCE THEY WON EVERYWHERE, DID EUROPE BECOME ALL VIKING THEN?
WELL, ACTUALLY IT WAS RATHER THE VIKINGS WHO BECAME EUROPEANIZED AND BLENDED IN WITH THE OTHERS...

BY SETTLING IN AND JOINING FORCES WITH KINGS AND EMPERORS, THEY QUICKLY LOST THEIR OWN CULTURE.

WILLIAM LONGSWORD, DUKE OF NORMANDY AND ROLAND'S SON, COULDN'T FIND ANYONE TO TEACH HIS OWN SON "OLD NORSE," THE VIKING LANGUAGE.

THEY RENOUNCED THEIR RELIGION FOR CHRISTIANITY, TOO.

FROM HAVING BEEN INVADERS, THEY BECAME THE PROTECTORS OF THE KINGDOMS OF EUROPE.
VIKINGS WHO WERE ESTABLISHED THERE EVEN REPELLED RAIDS BY THE OTHER VIKINGS THAT KEPT COMING FROM THE NORTH!
THEY DIDN'T STICK TOGETHER?
NOPE! THEY PROTECTED THEIR NEW LANDS!
THE VIKINGS' DESCENDANTS REMAINED POWERFUL WARRIORS: WILLIAM LONGSWORDS' GREAT-GREAT-GRANDSON CONQUERED ENGLAND IN 1066.
SO THEY CALLED HIM WILLIAM THE CONQUEROR!

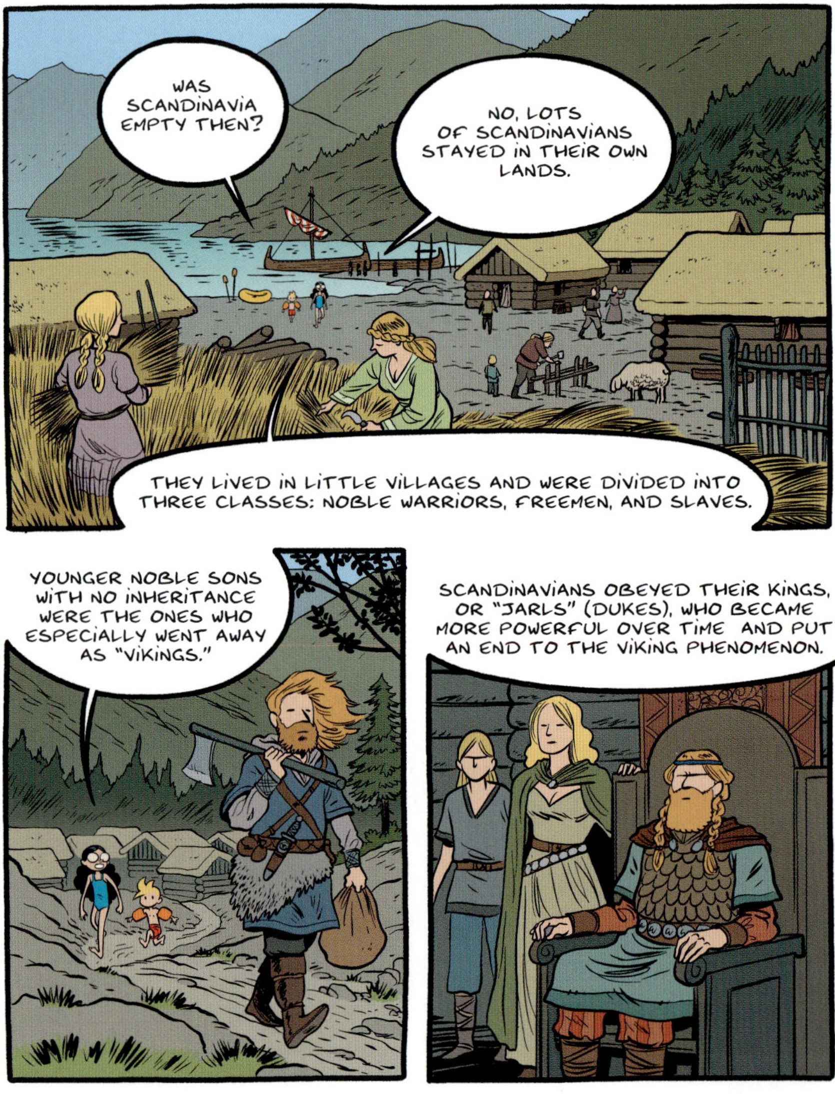

WAS SCANDINAVIA EMPTY THEN?

NO, LOTS OF SCANDINAVIANS STAYED IN THEIR OWN LANDS.

THEY LIVED IN LITTLE VILLAGES AND WERE DIVIDED INTO THREE CLASSES: NOBLE WARRIORS, FREEMEN, AND SLAVES.

STARTING IN THE 11TH CENTURY, THE SCANDINAVIAN PEOPLE WERE UNITED INTO THREE LARGE KINGDOMS: SWEDEN, NORWAY, AND DENMARK.
THEY STILL EXIST TODAY.

THEIR CHRISTIAN KINGS WOULD NOT ACCEPT VIKING EXPEDITIONS THAT DIDN'T OBEY THEM AND THAT THREATENED ALLIED NATIONS.

ALSO, THE EUROPEAN KINGDOMS WERE BETTER PROTECTED AND GRADUALLY THE ATTACKS CEASED.

IT WAS THE END OF THE VIKING ERA, WHICH HAD LASTED ABOUT THREE CENTURIES...

BUT IF THE VIKINGS "MELTED" INTO THE EUROPEAN POPULATION, HOW DO WE KNOW ABOUT THEIR ADVENTURES?
WELL, SCANDINAVIAN POETS WROTE GREAT "SAGAS"!
VIKINGS

WRITTEN SEVERAL CENTURIES LATER, THESE BOOKS TOLD THE TALES OF THEIR EPICS...

SOME SAGAS WERE LEGENDARY, SUCH AS THAT OF THE HERO **SIGURD**...
WHAT DID HE DO?

HE WAS SAID TO HAVE KILLED THE DRAGON **FAFNIR**, BECOMING INVINCIBLE AFTER BATHING HIMSELF IN ITS BLOOD!

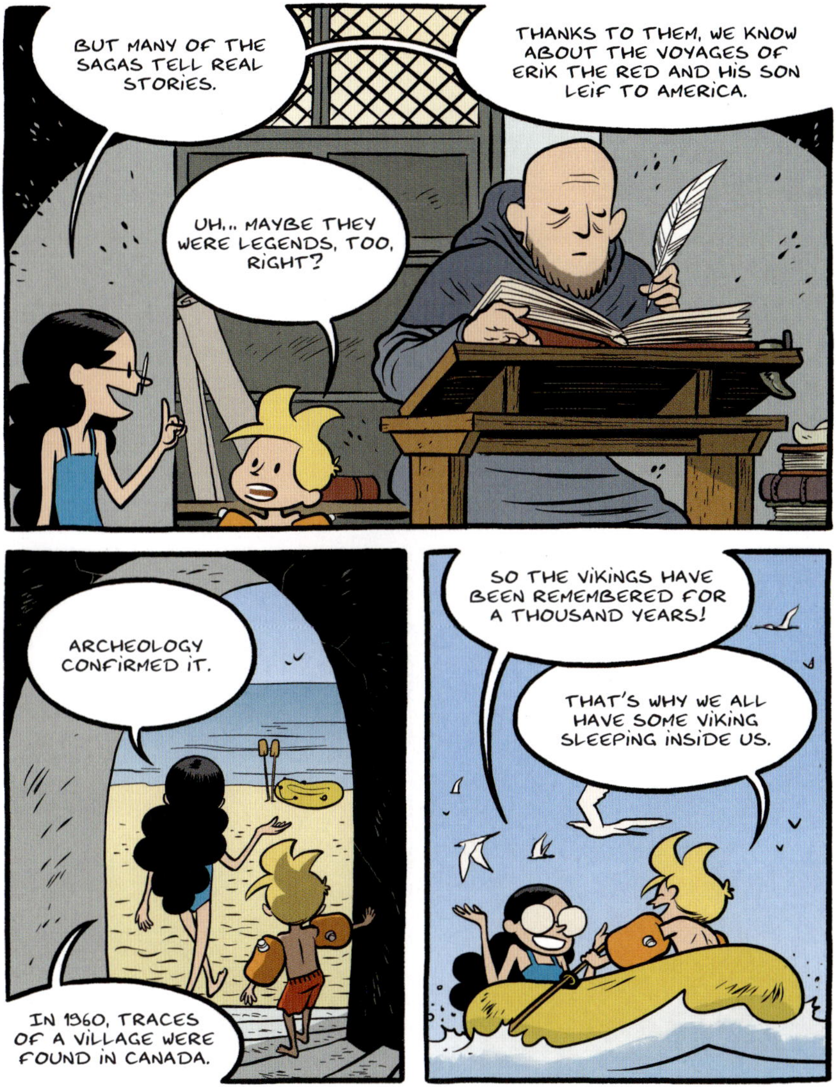

BUT MANY OF THE SAGAS TELL REAL STORIES.
THANKS TO THEM, WE KNOW ABOUT THE VOYAGES OF ERIK THE RED AND HIS SON LEIF TO AMERICA.
UH... MAYBE THEY WERE LEGENDS, TOO, RIGHT?

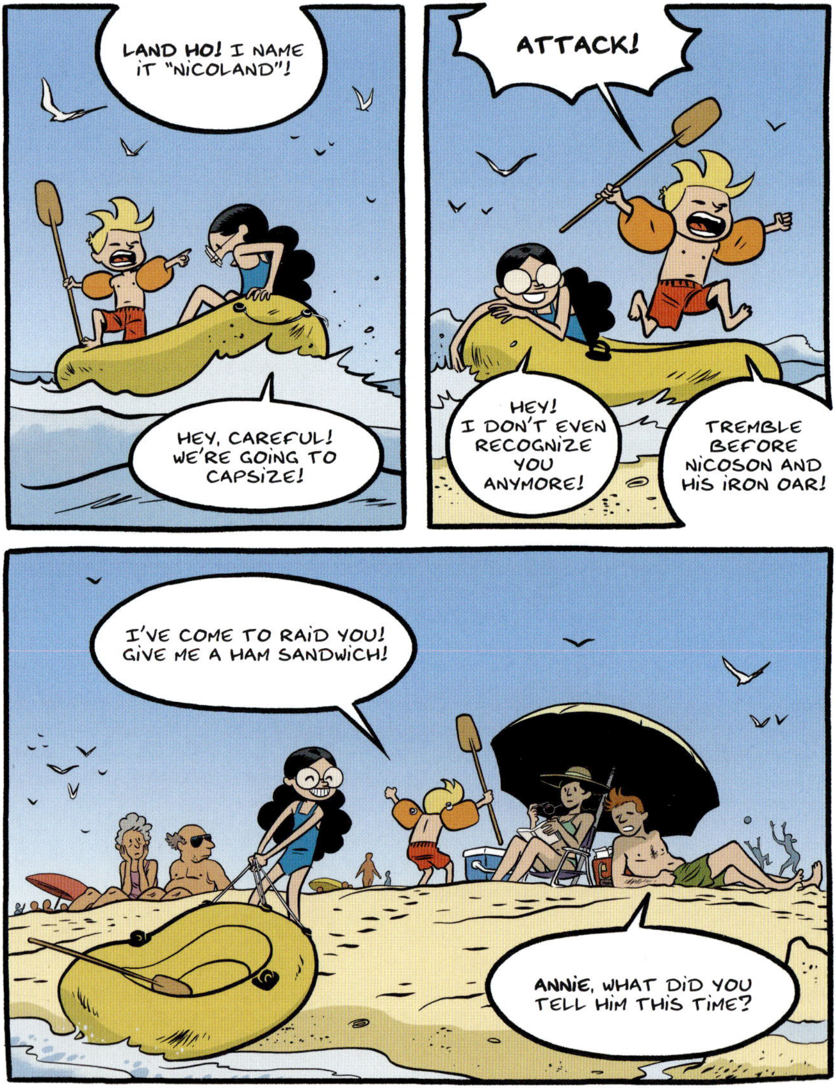

I'VE COME TO RAID YOU! GIVE ME A HAM SANDWICH!

ANNIE, WHAT DID YOU TELL HIM THIS TIME?

And there's more...

Some people who made history...

Erik the Red
(c. 950 - c. 1003)

Erik Thorvaldson, named for the color of his hair and his beard, Erik the Red was the son of a Norwegian who settled in Iceland. After being accused of murder, he was forced to leave the island and went to sea westward. Erik explored the coasts of a land he named Groenland ("Green land"). Around 985, he organized the colonization of this new land, which would be occupied by the Vikings for about 450 years, and he became the paramount chieftain of the colony. We know his story from the saga *Erik the Red.*

Leif Erikson
(c. 970 - c. 1020)

The son of Erik the Red who settled in Groenland, Leif continued maritime exploration to the West. During his journey, Leif discovered several lands that he named Helluland ("land of flat rocks"), Markland ("land of forest") and Vinland ("land of vines"). This was the first time a European reached the American continent. Leif did not stay in these new lands: he returned to Groenland to take over from his father as paramount chieftain of the Viking colony until his death.

Rurik
(c. 830 - 879)

The Eastern European Slavic tribes invited Varingian Viking chief Rurik to lead them and put an end to their constant wars. In 862, he settled in Novgorod, a city in the north of today's Russia, conquering enough land to assure his power. He is considered the founder of Kyivan Rus, the country consisting of the collected territories of the Rus (Vikings) that moved to the East. This state persisted until 1240 under the authority of Rurik's descendants, who then became the princes of Moscow and tsars of Russia until 1598.

Cnut the Great
(995 - 1025)

When he was 18, Cnut went to conquer England with his father, then King of Denmark. In 1016, after hard fighting, Cnut became the King of England and entrusted the lands of Great Britain to the Viking "jarls" (counts) who were his allies. In 1018, he became the King of Denmark; ten years later, he began his conquest of Norway. At that point, Cnut ruled an immense region consisting of England, Denmark, and Norway. But upon his death, his kingdom was split up.

Ships and Navigators

The Vikings primarily used oak or pine wood to **build ships**. They had to find huge trees in order to make the keel—sort of a boat's spine—out of one piece. The boards were put together and sealed with wool, tar, and fat. The ships could be as long as 115 feet and hold 70 people.

Building a "Skip." A boat had different names depending on its size: snekkar, skeid, knarr, karvi, snekkja, dreki...

The **mast** could be removed, to avoid detection or to move by rowing. It was attached by a large piece of wood in the middle of the hull. The **figurehead**, often a dragon, could also be removed, so as not to frighten a friendly vessel.

Sailing in the "skips" wasn't easy: it was even dangerous. The Vikings spent as much of their time bailing out the water that came into the ships as they did rowing. Shipwrecks and drowning were common: when Erik the Red left to colonize Groenland, he took 25 ships with him but only 15 reached their destination.

Many Viking chieftains wanted to **stay with their ships after death.** Some were buried with their ships—which is how we discovered them; others were burned. They also departed this world with their weapons, and sometimes with one of their slaves, who were sacrificed next to them.

Discovery of a Viking tomb in Oseberg, Norway.

Gods and Legends

There were many Norse gods: **Odin**, the king, and his son, **Thor**, are the best known. But there was also Odin's wife, **Frigg**, who wove the clouds. **Freyr** and his sister **Freyja** were associated with fertility and beauty. **Loki** was a destructive god who would lead the battle at the end of time between the other gods and humans, Ragnarök.

Scandinavian myths were about nature and animals. The universe was said to be supported by a huge tree named **Yggdrasil**, which Odin's stronghold was built on. The earth was held up by a sea serpent, **Jörmungandr**, which was biting its own tail. **Skölll** and **Hati** were two wolf brothers who chased the sun and the moon and would catch them at the end of time, when their father, **Fenrir**, would devour Odin.

Scandinavians also thought the earth was populated by fantastic beings: elves, dwarves, trolls, and giants... These creatures could do magic and represented fearsome forces of nature. **Trolls**, for example, were supernaturally strong and hostile to humans. They lived in the seas, mountains, and forests.

Before 1000, Scandinavians used **runes** as a system of writing for all sorts of inscriptions, and particularly for **gravestones**. These had symbolic drawings on them, inspired by Odin himself, according to legend. As a result runes gained a reputation for being magical, which in reality they are not.

Timeline

793
First Viking raid led against the Lindisfarne monastery.

799
After the Vikings attacked the island of Noirmoutier, Charlemagne sets watches on all the coastlines of his empire.

911
Viking chieftain Roland gets Normandy.

Around 980
Erik the Red discovers Groenland.

988
The Byzantine emperor creates the "Varingian Guard."

Around 1000
Leif Erikson discovers Vinland in America.

865 — The "Great Viking Army" launches its first attacks on the British Isles.

Around 870 — The Vikings settle in Iceland.

Around 880 — Varingians found Kyivan Rus, which will become Russia.

885 — The Vikings besiege Paris.

1028 — Cnut the Great unifies Denmark, Norway, and England under his rule.

1066 — William the Conqueror invades England. The last event of the Viking era.

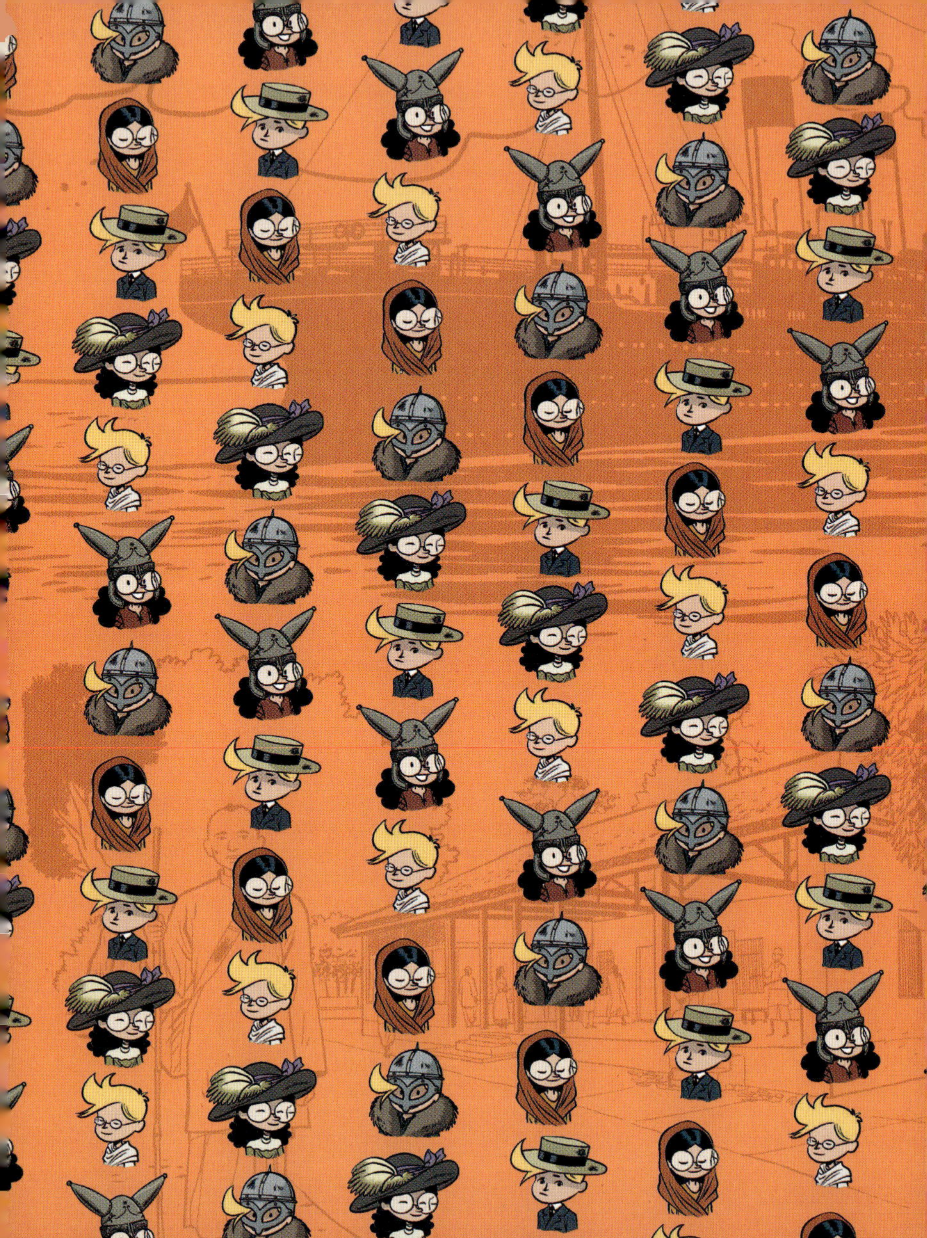

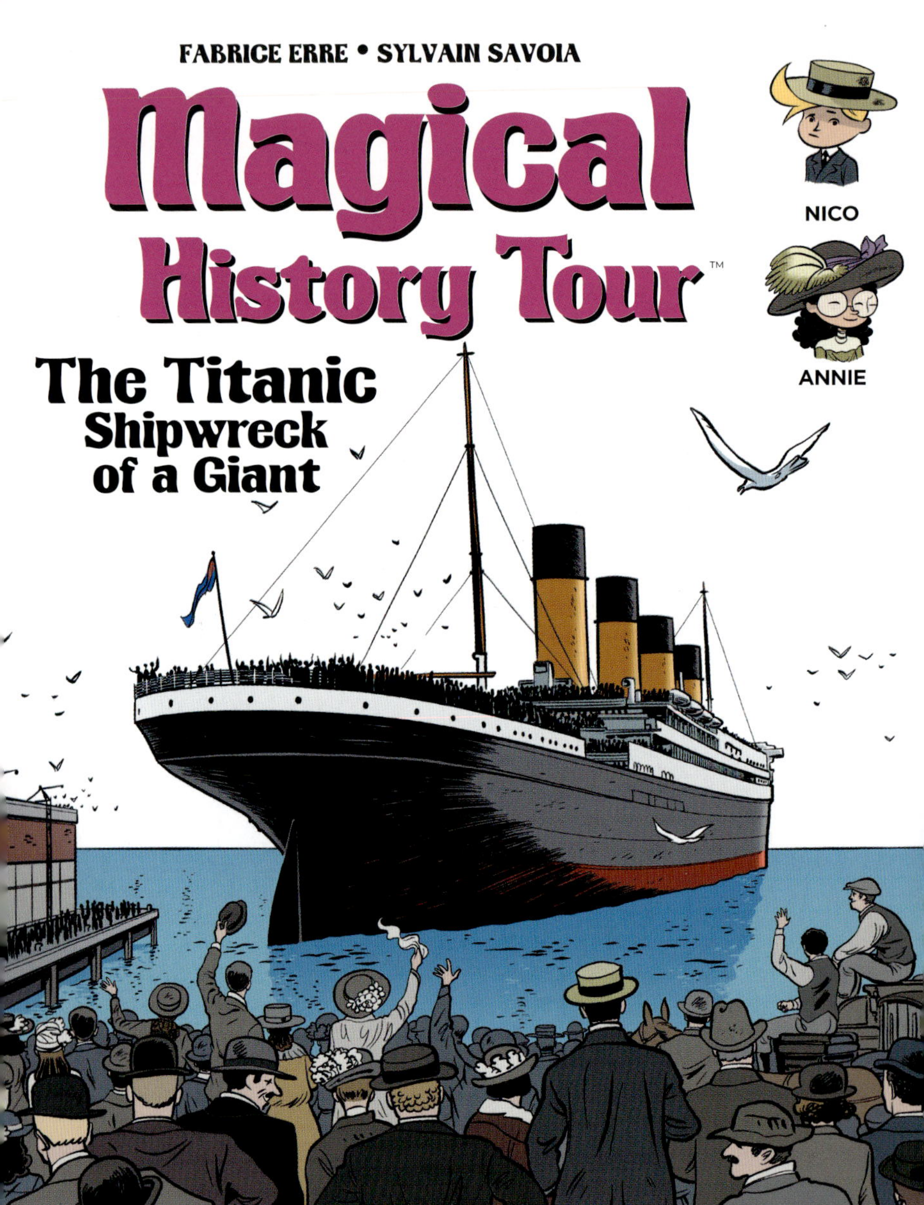
FABRICE ERRE • SYLVAIN SAVOIA
Magical History Tour™
The Titanic
Shipwreck of a Giant
NICO
ANNIE

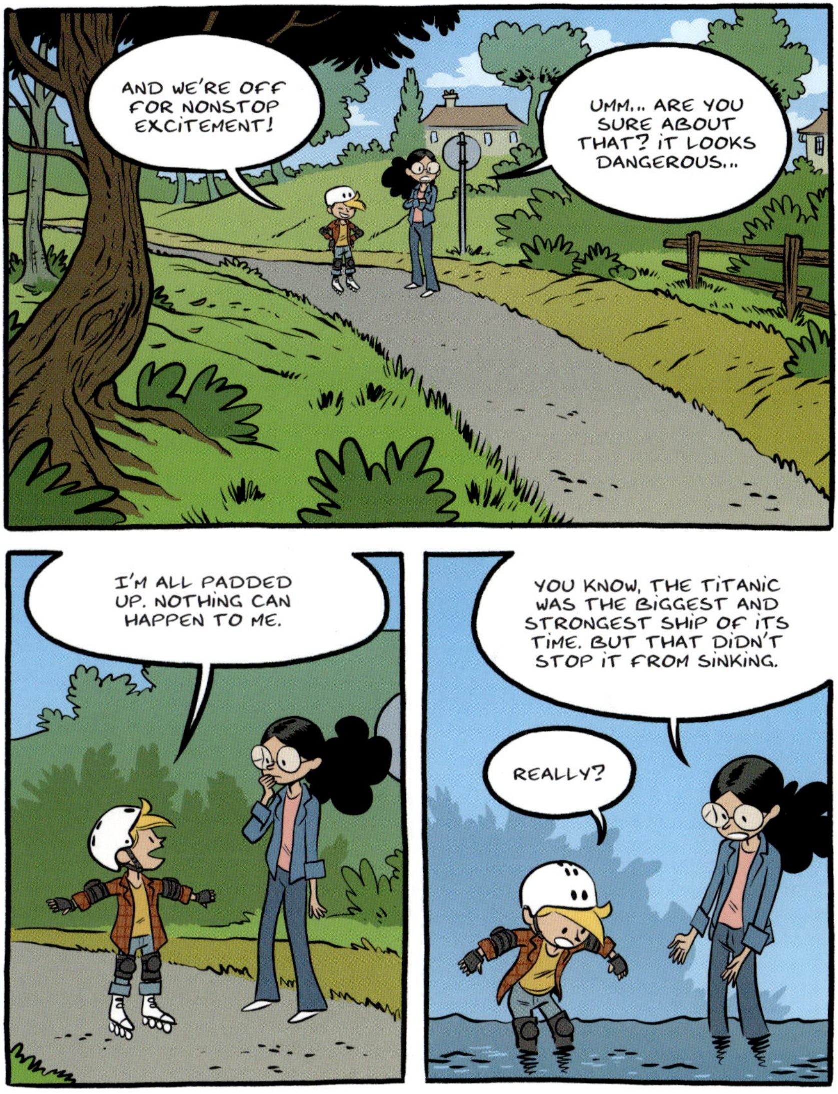

AND WE'RE OFF FOR NONSTOP EXCITEMENT!

UMM... ARE YOU SURE ABOUT THAT? IT LOOKS DANGEROUS...

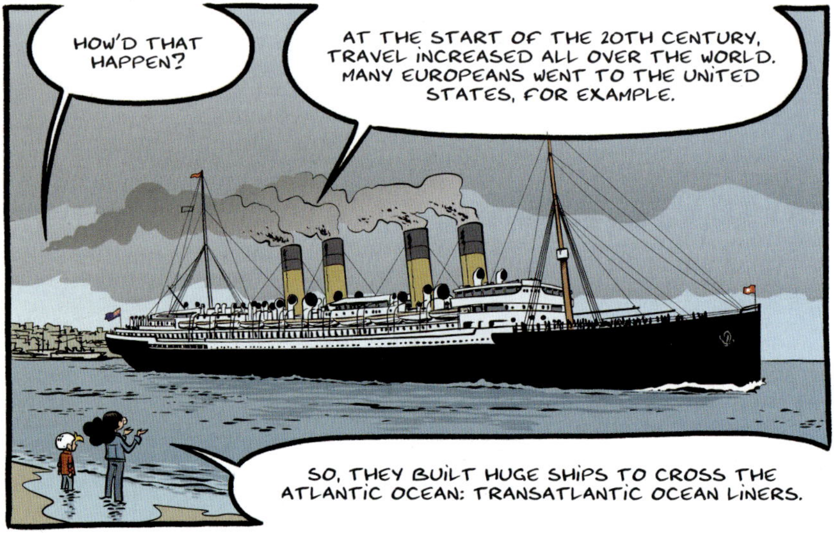

HOW'D THAT HAPPEN?

AT THE START OF THE 20TH CENTURY, TRAVEL INCREASED ALL OVER THE WORLD. MANY EUROPEANS WENT TO THE UNITED STATES, FOR EXAMPLE.

SO, THEY BUILT HUGE SHIPS TO CROSS THE ATLANTIC OCEAN: TRANSATLANTIC OCEAN LINERS.

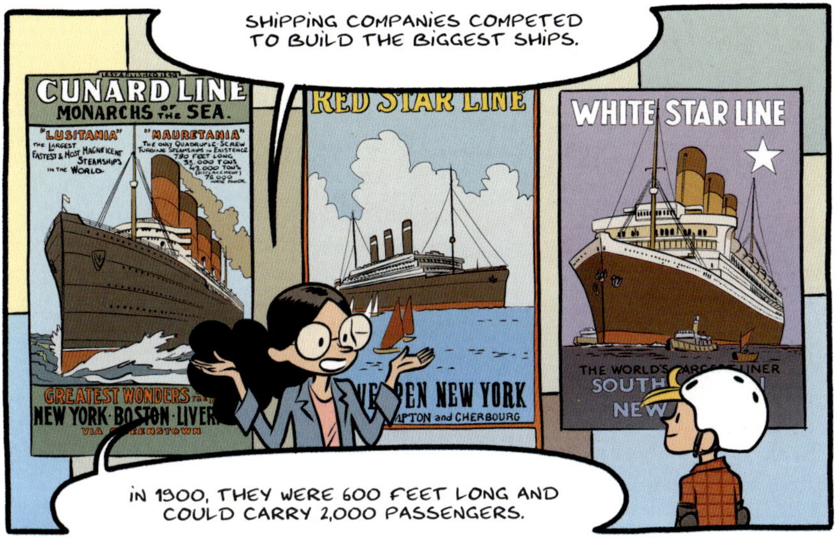

SHIPPING COMPANIES COMPETED TO BUILD THE BIGGEST SHIPS.

IN 1900, THEY WERE 600 FEET LONG AND COULD CARRY 2,000 PASSENGERS.

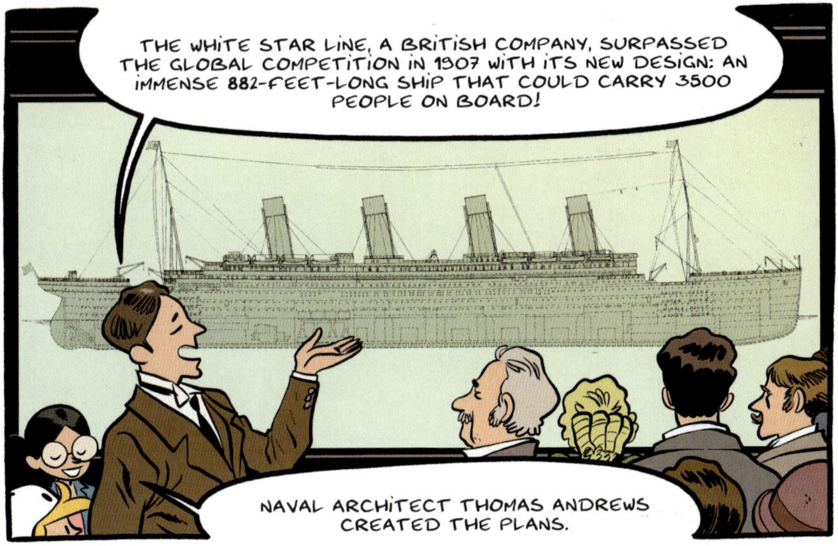

THE WHITE STAR LINE, A BRITISH COMPANY, SURPASSED THE GLOBAL COMPETITION IN 1907 WITH ITS NEW DESIGN: AN IMMENSE 882-FEET-LONG SHIP THAT COULD CARRY 3500 PEOPLE ON BOARD!

NAVAL ARCHITECT THOMAS ANDREWS CREATED THE PLANS.

THAT'S THE MODEL OF THE TITANIC?
YES, BUT THE TITANIC WAS ONE OF THREE SHIPS BUILT WITH THE SAME DESIGN: THE OLYMPIC AND THE BRITANNIC.
TITANIC
OLYMPIC
BRITANNIC
THE "MEGA-TRANSATLANTIC FAMILY" TRIPLETS!
THESE SHIPS WERE SUPPOSED TO BE THE BIGGEST, AND ALSO THE SAFEST, TO APPEAL TO PASSENGERS.
THERE WAS AN ULTRA-MODERN SYSTEM OF WATERTIGHT DOORS IN THE DOUBLE-BOTTOMED HULL TO AVOID SINKING IF THERE WAS A LEAK.
THE TITANIC WAS DESIGNED TO BE **UNSINKABLE**: IT COULDN'T GO UNDER!

THE TITANIC AND THE OLYMPIC WERE BUILT AT A SHIPYARD IN IRELAND AT THE SAME TIME, STARTING IN 1909.
THEY HAD TO BUILD AN ENORMOUS GANTRY CRANE AND EMPLOYED MORE THAN 11,000 WORKERS.
THE HULL WAS ASSEMBLED COMPLETELY BEFORE BEING PUT IN THE WATER TO FINISH THE INTERIOR.
OH! LOOK AT THE SIZE OF THAT PROPELLER!
THE TITANIC HAD THREE OF THEM, POWERED BY HUGE STEAM ENGINES THAT BURNED COAL.

THE OLYMPIC WAS FINISHED FIRST, IN 1911, THEN THE TITANIC IN 1912. THE BRITANNIC WOULD BE FINISHED IN 1914.
THE TITANIC'S INITIAL VOYAGE, WHICH WAS SUPPOSED TO GO TO NEW YORK, WAS AN EVENT: THOUSANDS OF PEOPLE ATTENDED ITS DEPARTURE.
LEADING FIGURES, SUCH AS THE DIRECTOR OF THE WHITE STAR LINE, **JOSEPH BRUCE ISMAY**, TOOK PART.
EDWARD JOHN SMITH, THE MOST EXPERIENCED CAPTAIN IN THE COMPANY, COMMANDED THE SHIP. THE SHIP'S DESIGNER, **THOMAS ANDREWS**, WAS ALSO ON BOARD.
THAT BUILT CONFIDENCE!

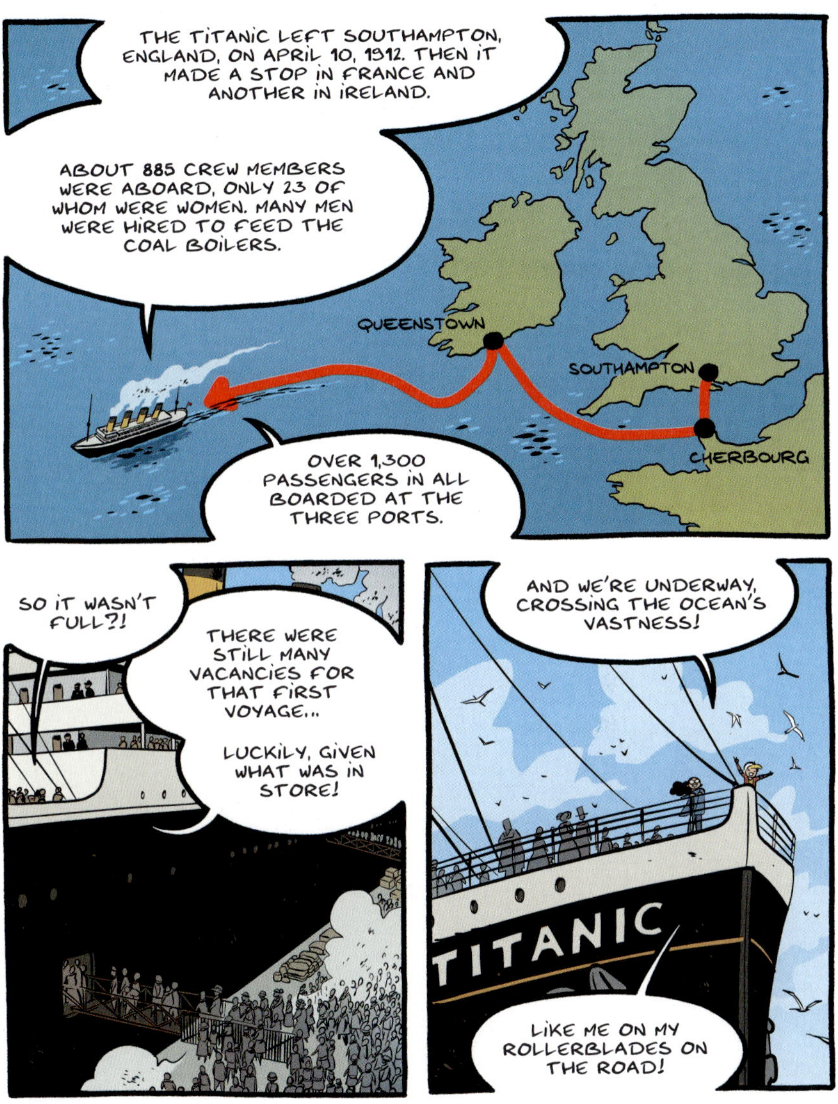

THE TITANIC LEFT SOUTHAMPTON, ENGLAND, ON APRIL 10, 1912. THEN IT MADE A STOP IN FRANCE AND ANOTHER IN IRELAND.

ABOUT 885 CREW MEMBERS WERE ABOARD, ONLY 23 OF WHOM WERE WOMEN. MANY MEN WERE HIRED TO FEED THE COAL BOILERS.

QUEENSTOWN

SOUTHAMPTON

CHERBOURG

OVER 1,300 PASSENGERS IN ALL BOARDED AT THE THREE PORTS.

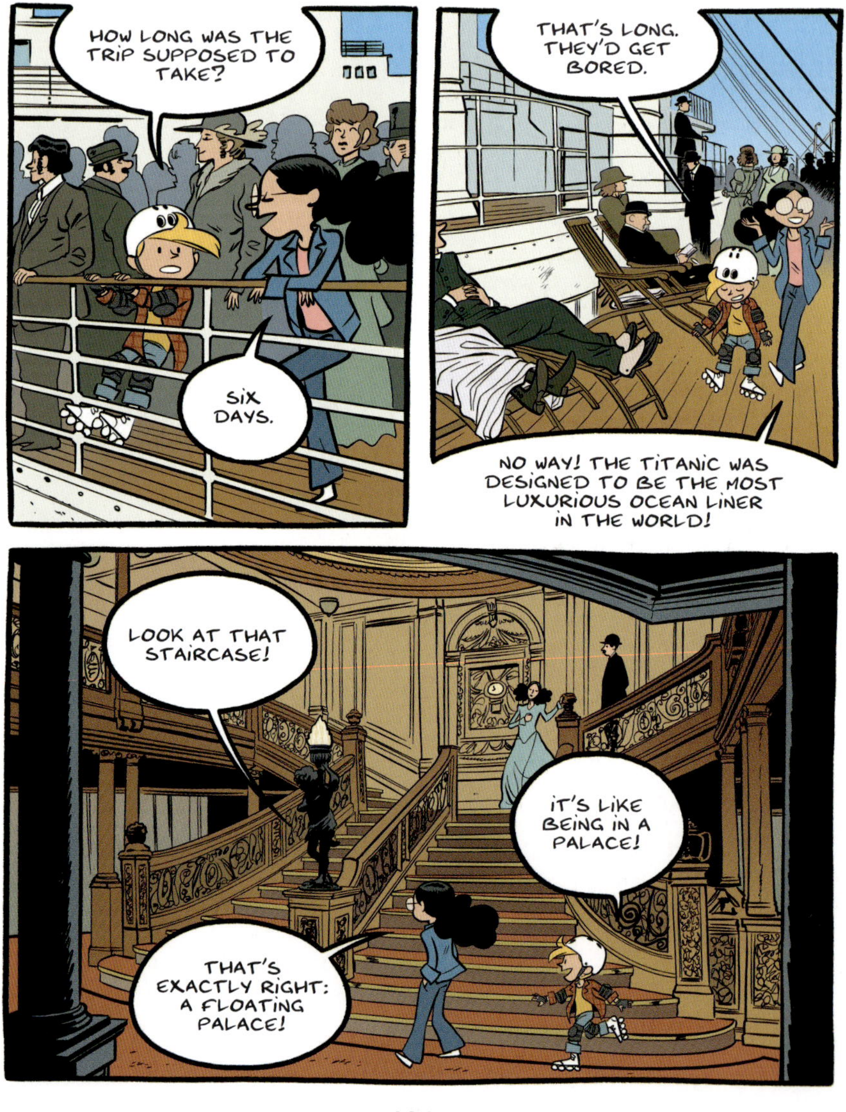

LOOK AT THAT STAIRCASE!

IT'S LIKE BEING IN A PALACE!

THAT'S EXACTLY RIGHT: A FLOATING PALACE!

FIRST-CLASS CABINS WERE MAGNIFICENT...

EVERYTHING WAS DESIGNED FOR COMFORT: A RESTAURANT...

PROMENADE DECKS...
HEY! THEY COULD GO ROLLER-BLADING!
AH, YES. BUT THEY CALLED IT ROLLER SKATING BACK THEN.

THERE WAS EVEN A POOL!
WOW!

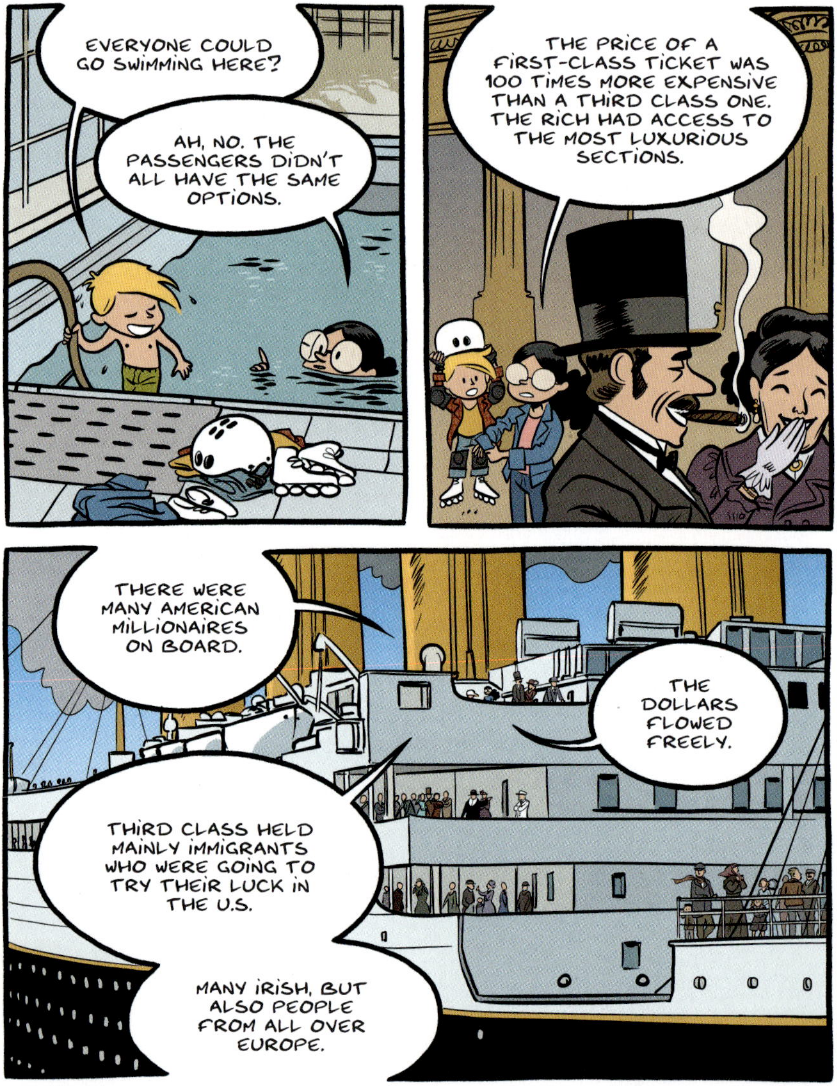

THERE WERE MANY AMERICAN MILLIONAIRES ON BOARD.

THE DOLLARS FLOWED FREELY.

THIRD CLASS HELD MAINLY IMMIGRANTS WHO WERE GOING TO TRY THEIR LUCK IN THE U.S.

MANY IRISH, BUT ALSO PEOPLE FROM ALL OVER EUROPE.

THEY DIDN'T MINGLE?

NO, THEY OCCUPIED DIFFERENT PARTS OF THE SHIP, AWAY FROM EACH OTHER...

FIRST CLASS HAD FANCY PARTIES UP TOP...

WHILE THE IMMIGRANTS GOT TOGETHER DOWN BELOW TO PLAY MUSIC FROM THEIR HOME COUNTRIES.

FOR FIVE DAYS, THE CROSSING WAS IDYLLIC FOR EVERYONE...

NOTHING COULD HAPPEN TO THE BIGGEST SHIP IN THE WORLD.

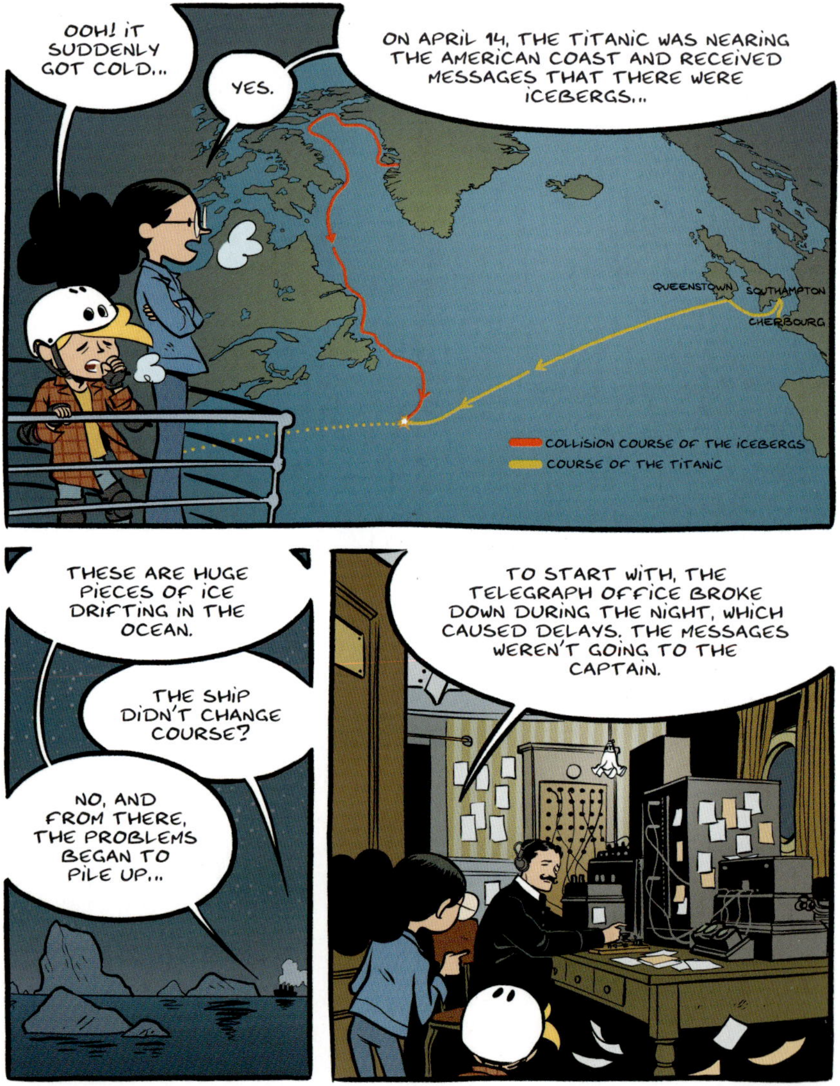

OOH! IT SUDDENLY GOT COLD...
YES.
ON APRIL 14, THE TITANIC WAS NEARING THE AMERICAN COAST AND RECEIVED MESSAGES THAT THERE WERE ICEBERGS...
QUEENSTOWN
SOUTHAMPTON
CHERBOURG
COLLISION COURSE OF THE ICEBERGS
COURSE OF THE TITANIC

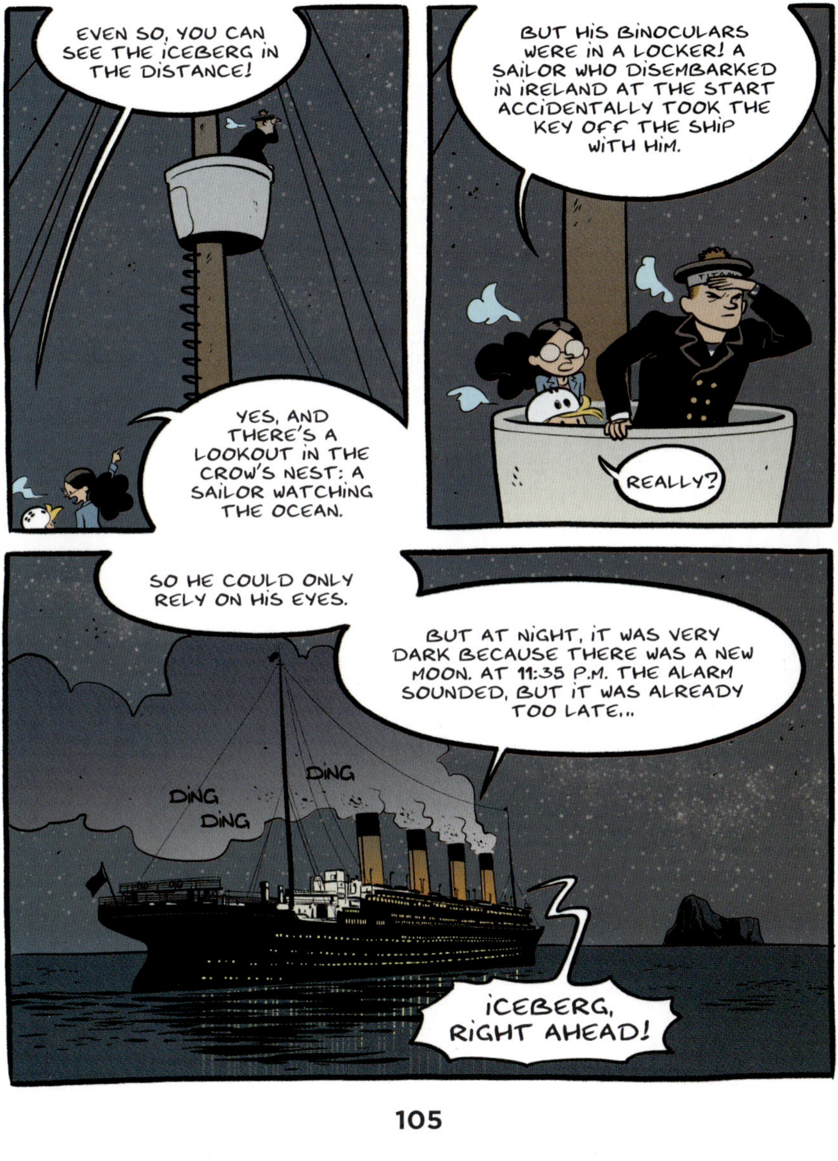

SO HE COULD ONLY RELY ON HIS EYES.

BUT AT NIGHT, IT WAS VERY DARK BECAUSE THERE WAS A NEW MOON. AT 11:35 P.M. THE ALARM SOUNDED, BUT IT WAS ALREADY TOO LATE...

DING

DING

DING

ICEBERG, RIGHT AHEAD!

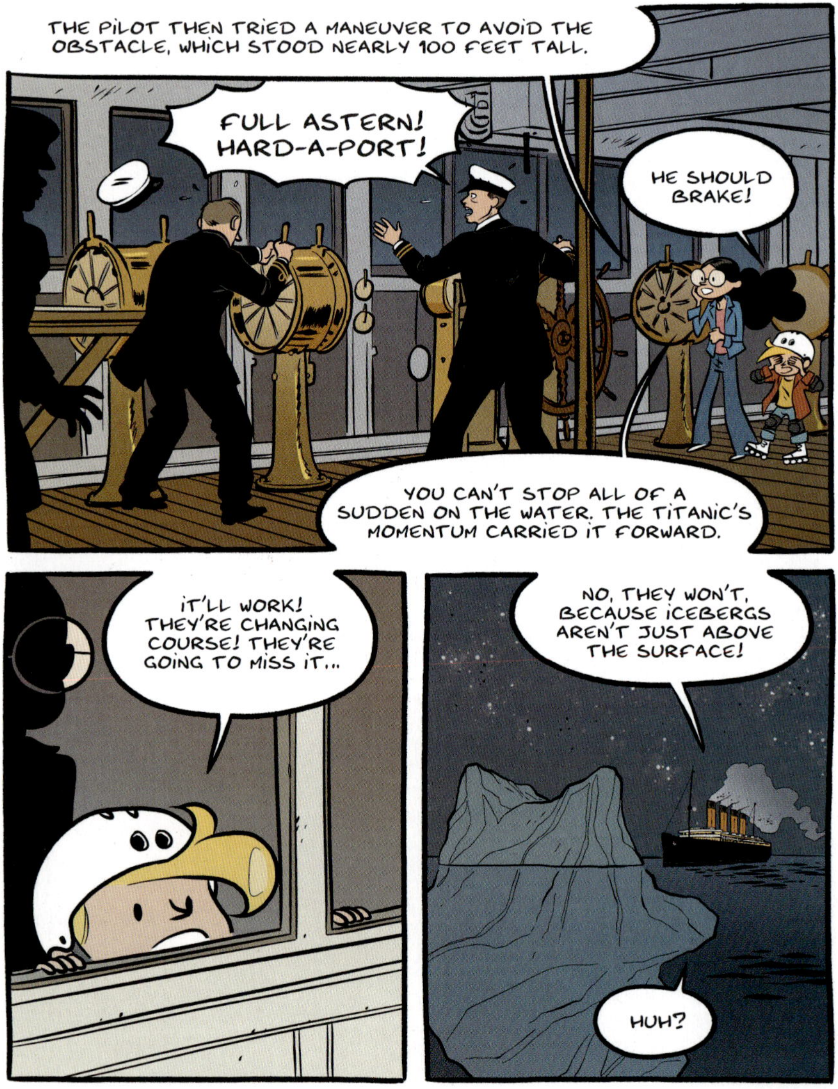

THE PILOT THEN TRIED A MANEUVER TO AVOID THE OBSTACLE, WHICH STOOD NEARLY 100 FEET TALL.

FULL ASTERN! HARD-A-PORT!

HE SHOULD BRAKE!

YOU CAN'T STOP ALL OF A SUDDEN ON THE WATER. THE TITANIC'S MOMENTUM CARRIED IT FORWARD.

THEY'RE HUGE UNDER THE WATER...
APRIL 14, 1912, 11:40 P.M.: COLLISION.
CRAAAAAAC
AAAAAAAH!
HANG ON!

-OOF!- MORE SCARY THAN PAINFUL. NOTHING LOOKS BROKEN...
THE DAMAGE WASN'T VISIBLE FROM HERE... BUT IT WAS QUITE SERIOUS!

THE HULL HAD "SCRAPED" AGAINST THE ICEBERG! IT RIPPED MORE THAN 230 FEET, ALL BELOW THE WATERLINE!

ICE CAN TEAR STEEL?
YES, THE IMPACT WAS HUGE! THE TITANIC WAS 57,320 TONS MOVING AT 25 MPH!

THE RIVETS- A TYPE OF NAIL THAT HOLDS THE HULL'S METAL PLATES TOGETHER - DIDN'T HOLD...
WATER GUSHED IN.

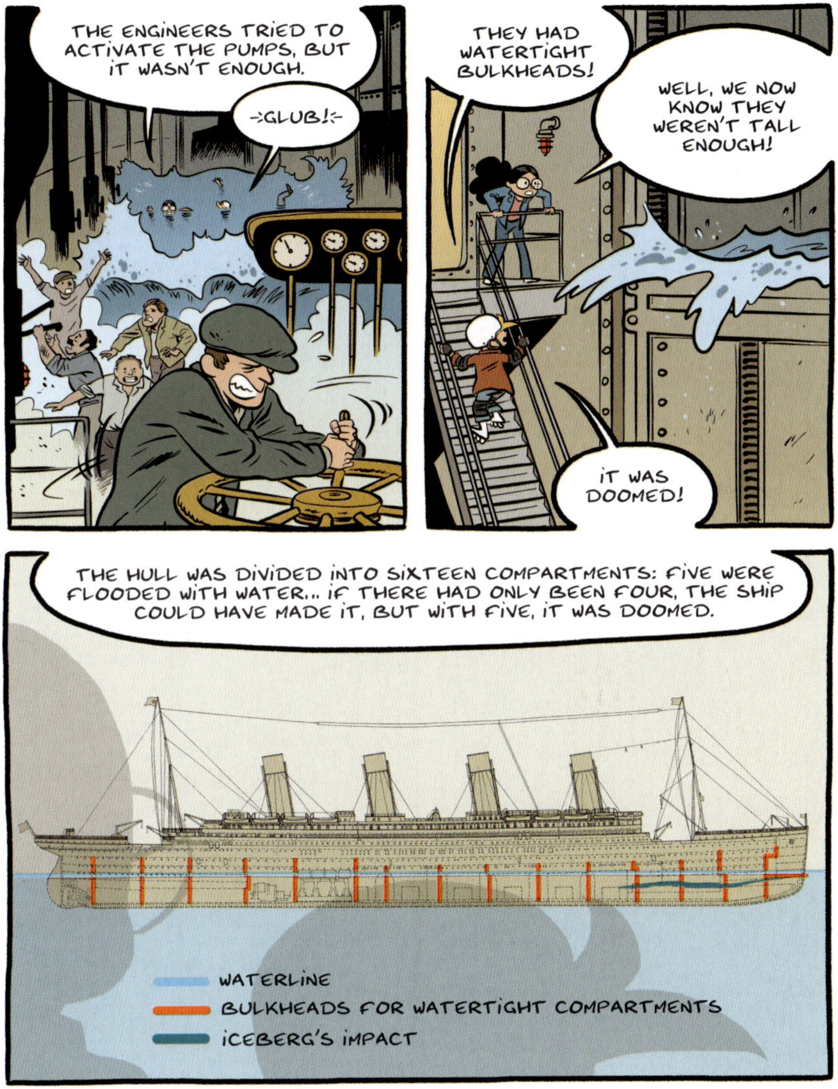

THE HULL WAS DIVIDED INTO SIXTEEN COMPARTMENTS: FIVE WERE FLOODED WITH WATER... IF THERE HAD ONLY BEEN FOUR, THE SHIP COULD HAVE MADE IT, BUT WITH FIVE, IT WAS DOOMED.

WATERLINE

BULKHEADS FOR WATERTIGHT COMPARTMENTS

ICEBERG'S IMPACT

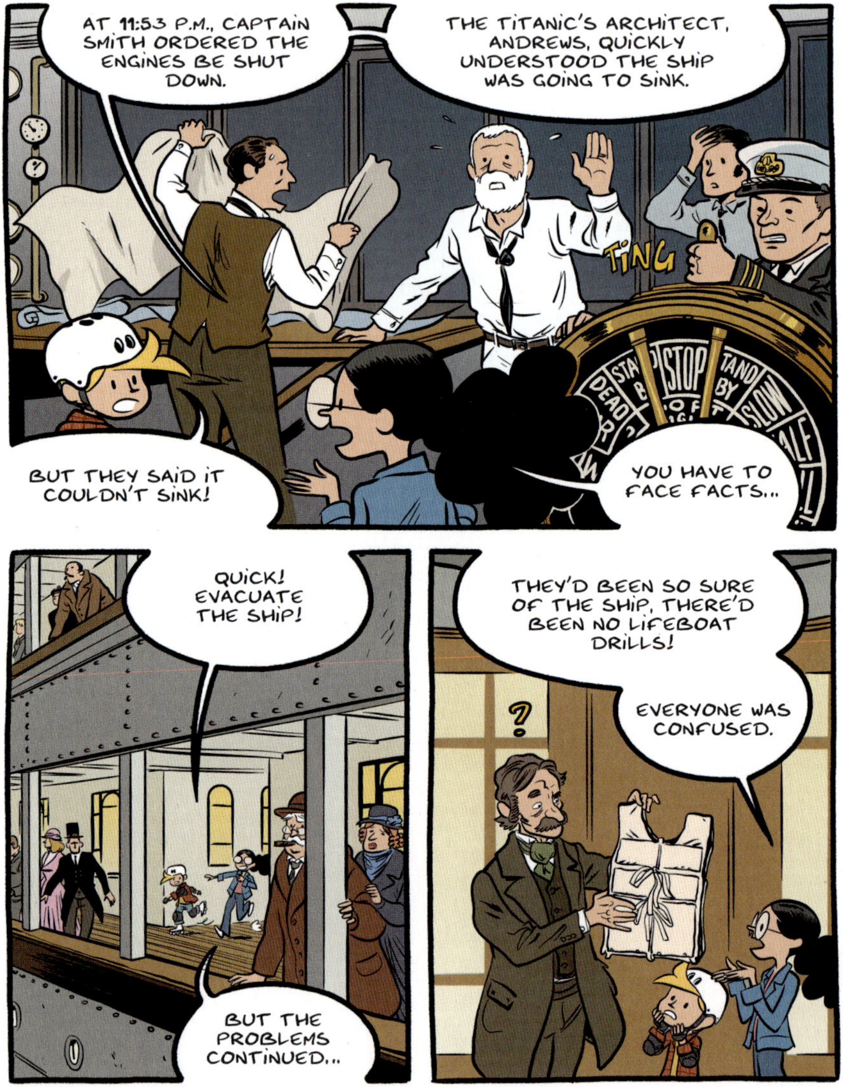

AT 11:53 P.M., CAPTAIN SMITH ORDERED THE ENGINES BE SHUT DOWN.

THE TITANIC'S ARCHITECT, ANDREWS, QUICKLY UNDERSTOOD THE SHIP WAS GOING TO SINK.

TING

BUT THEY SAID IT COULDN'T SINK!

YOU HAVE TO FACE FACTS...

AND MOST OF ALL, THERE WEREN'T ENOUGH LIFEBOATS TO CARRY ALL THE PASSENGERS!

THE LIFEBOATS WERE INTENDED TO TRANSPORT TRAVELERS TO ANOTHER SHIP IN CASE OF A PROBLEM...

WHAT?!

NOT TO SIMULTANEOUSLY CARRY EVERYONE TO SAFETY!

UNFORTUNATELY, NO OTHER SHIP WAS THERE...

THE NEAREST, THE CALIFORNIAN, WAS BLOCKED BY THE ICE. BUT ITS RADIO OPERATOR HAD GONE TO BED!

CALIFORNIAN

HE DIDN'T HEAR THE TITANIC'S DISTRESS CALLS...

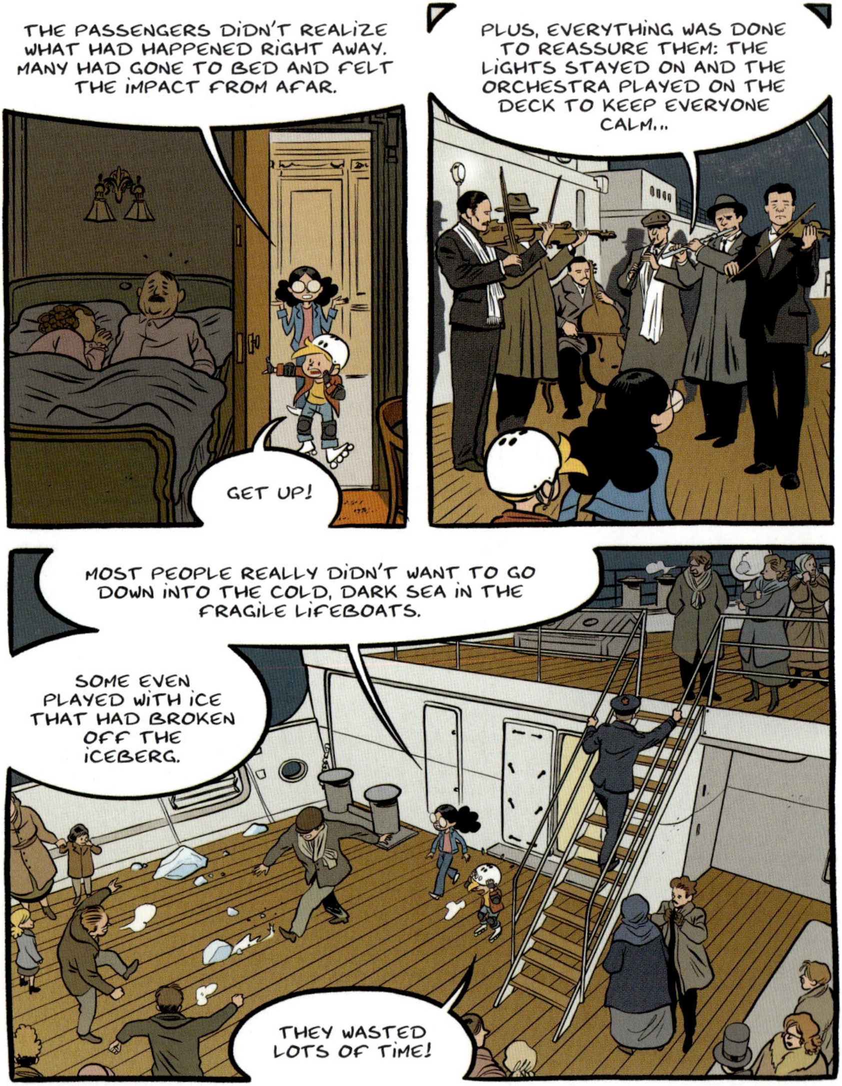

MOST PEOPLE REALLY DIDN'T WANT TO GO DOWN INTO THE COLD, DARK SEA IN THE FRAGILE LIFEBOATS.

SOME EVEN PLAYED WITH ICE THAT HAD BROKEN OFF THE ICEBERG.

THEY WASTED LOTS OF TIME!

AT 12:45 A.M., THE FIRST LIFEBOATS LEFT WITH VERY FEW PEOPLE ON BOARD.

WOMEN AND CHILDREN FIRST!

UH, SO WE CAN GO...

THOSE IN FIRST CLASS WERE CALMLY EVACUATED FIRST.
BUT THOSE IN SECOND AND PARTICULARLY THIRD CLASS GOT LESS INFORMATION.
THEY HAD A LONGER WAY TO GO TO GET TO THE LIFEBOATS! AND SOME OF THEM WERE TRAPPED BEHIND THE GATES SEPARATING THE CLASSES...
SOME PASSENGERS TRIED TO JUMP INTO THE LIFEBOATS WHEN THEY WERE LOWERED.
OTHERS DOVE INTO THE WATER.

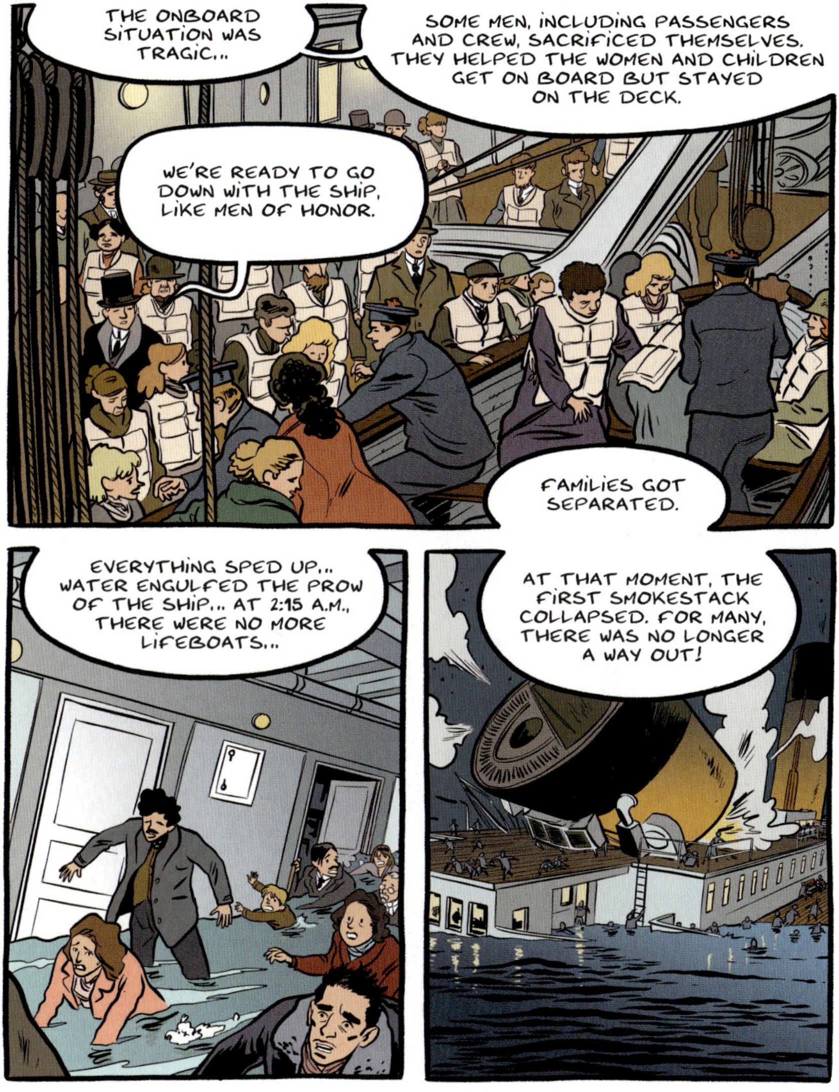

THE ONBOARD SITUATION WAS TRAGIC...

SOME MEN, INCLUDING PASSENGERS AND CREW, SACRIFICED THEMSELVES. THEY HELPED THE WOMEN AND CHILDREN GET ON BOARD BUT STAYED ON THE DECK.

WE'RE READY TO GO DOWN WITH THE SHIP, LIKE MEN OF HONOR.

FAMILIES GOT SEPARATED.

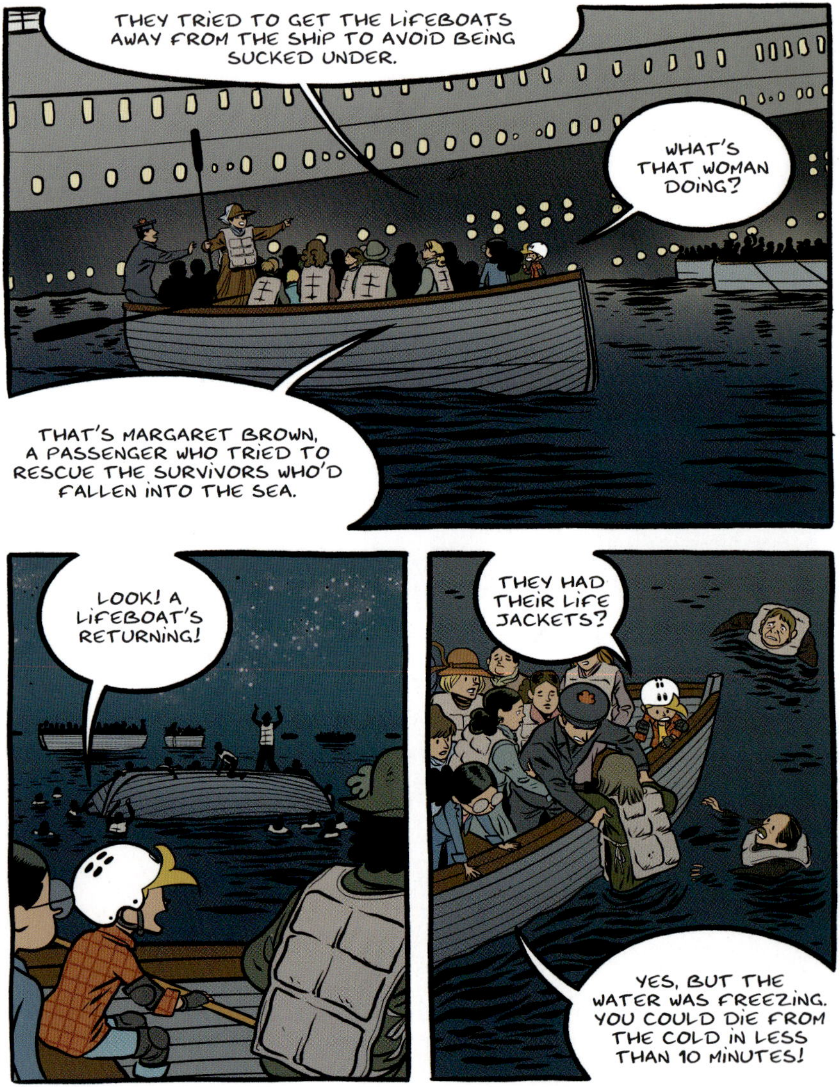

THEY TRIED TO GET THE LIFEBOATS AWAY FROM THE SHIP TO AVOID BEING SUCKED UNDER.

WHAT'S THAT WOMAN DOING?

THAT'S MARGARET BROWN, A PASSENGER WHO TRIED TO RESCUE THE SURVIVORS WHO'D FALLEN INTO THE SEA.

THERE WAS NOTHING THAT COULD BE DONE FOR THE TITANIC AS IT SANK.
AT 2:20 A.M., THE REAR OF THE SHIP ROSE UP; THE LIGHTS WENT OUT...
THEN THE SHIP BROKE IN TWO AND DISAPPEARED INTO THE WAVES.
HOW AWFUL!

CAN WE ROW BACK TO PORT?
IT'S MUCH TOO FAR!

OUR ONLY HOPE IS FOR A SHIP TO COME SAVE US.
HOW CAN WE ALERT THEM?

THE CARPATHIA HEARD THE DISTRESS CALLS BUT WOULDN'T ARRIVE UNTIL 4:00 A.M..

THEY MUSTN'T MISS US!
THAT'S WHY THEY FIRED DISTRESS FLARES.

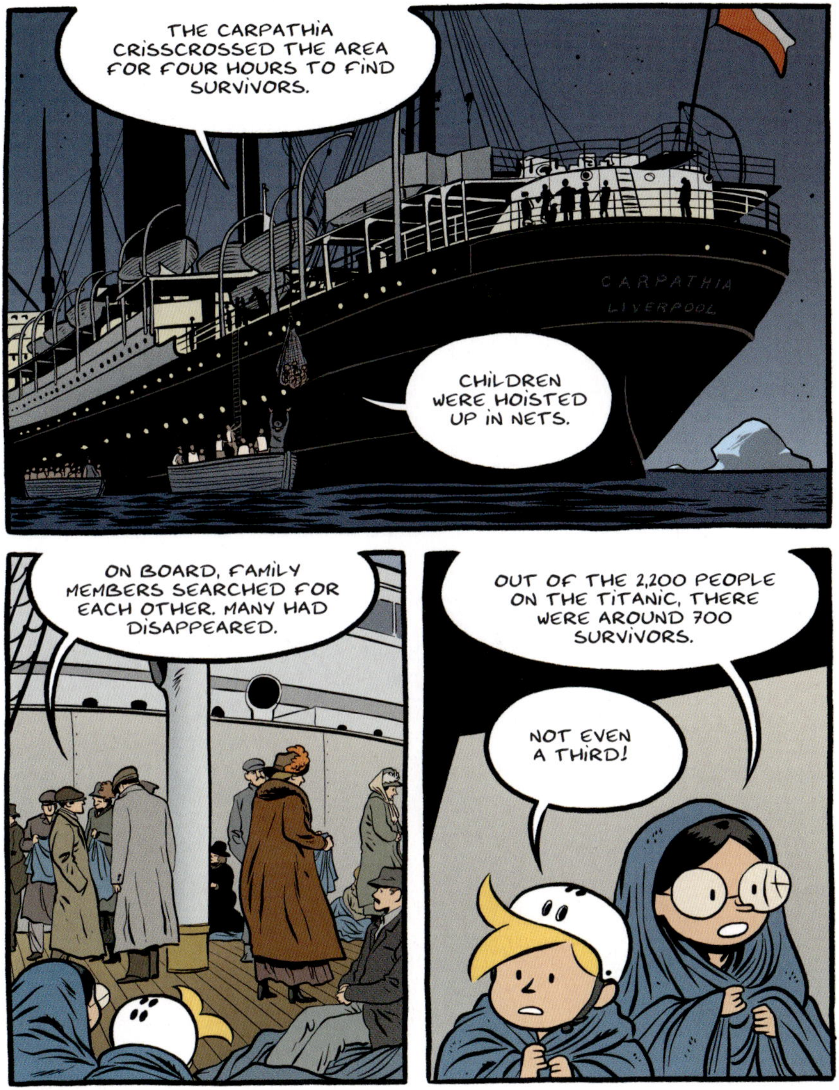

THE CARPATHIA CRISSCROSSED THE AREA FOR FOUR HOURS TO FIND SURVIVORS.

CARPATHIA
LIVERPOOL

CHILDREN WERE HOISTED UP IN NETS.

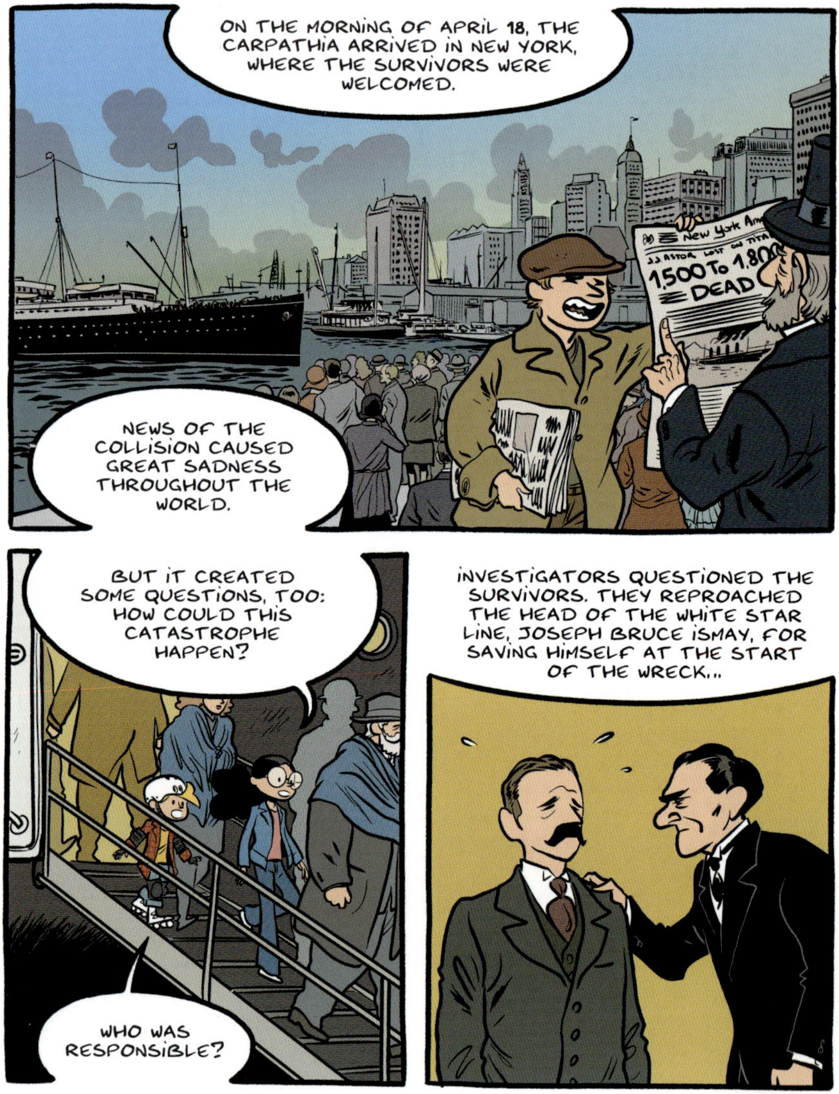

ON THE MORNING OF APRIL 18, THE CARPATHIA ARRIVED IN NEW YORK, WHERE THE SURVIVORS WERE WELCOMED.

NEWS OF THE COLLISION CAUSED GREAT SADNESS THROUGHOUT THE WORLD.

INVESTIGATORS QUESTIONED THE SURVIVORS. THEY REPROACHED THE HEAD OF THE WHITE STAR LINE, JOSEPH BRUCE ISMAY, FOR SAVING HIMSELF AT THE START OF THE WRECK...

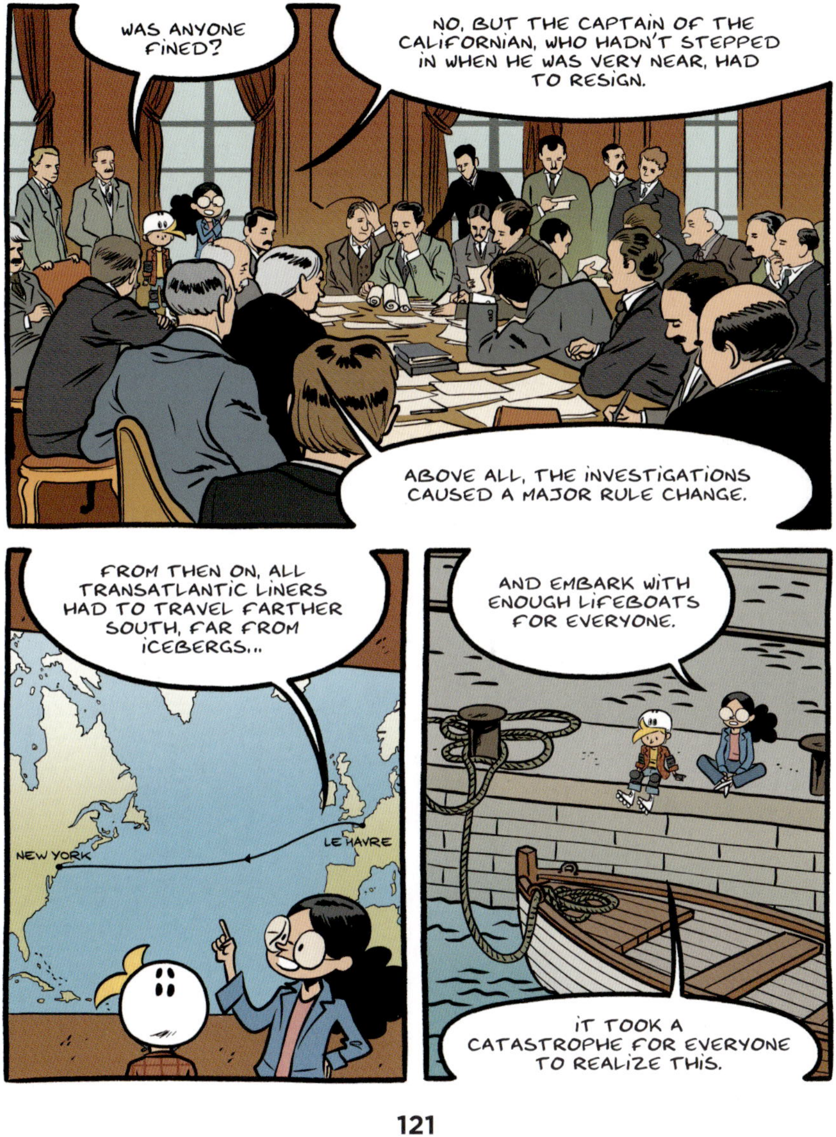

WAS ANYONE FINED?

NO, BUT THE CAPTAIN OF THE CALIFORNIAN, WHO HADN'T STEPPED IN WHEN HE WAS VERY NEAR, HAD TO RESIGN.

ABOVE ALL, THE INVESTIGATIONS CAUSED A MAJOR RULE CHANGE.

THE SHIPWRECK BECAME LEGENDARY... ONE OF THE DEADLIEST IN HISTORY. MOST OF ALL, IT HAD SEEMED COMPLETELY IMPOSSIBLE...

THE BRITANNIC, ONE OF THE TITANIC'S FELLOW TRIPLET SHIPS, ALSO SANK, WHEN STRUCK BY A MINE DURING WORLD WAR I...

THE OLYMPIC SAILED UNTIL 1935 WITHOUT ANY PROBLEMS.

CRAZY LEGENDS CIRCULATED: SOME SAID THAT CAPTAIN SMITH, WHO DIED IN THE SHIPWRECK, HAD SURVIVED AND WOULD STAY HIDDEN FOR THE REST OF HIS LIFE...

THE TITANIC CARRIED MYSTERIES WITH IT TO A PLACE SO DEEP THAT IT STAYED UNDISCOVERED FOR A LONG TIME.

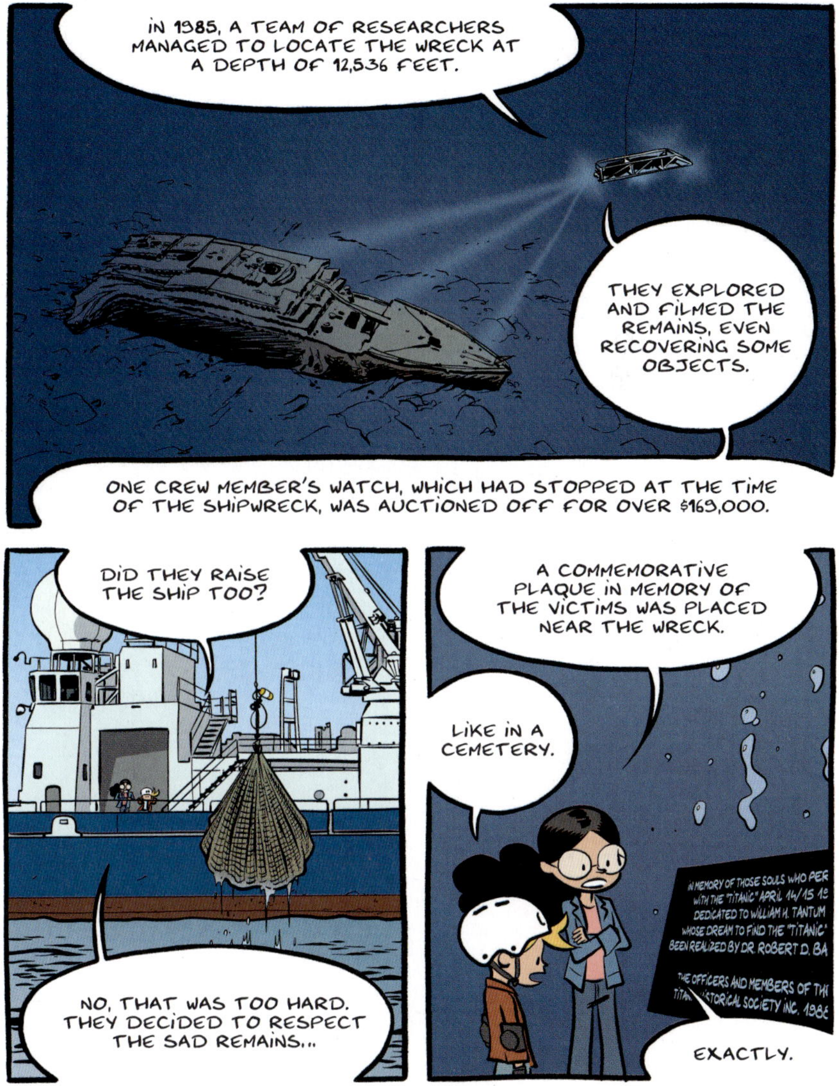

IN 1985, A TEAM OF RESEARCHERS MANAGED TO LOCATE THE WRECK AT A DEPTH OF 12,536 FEET.

THEY EXPLORED AND FILMED THE REMAINS, EVEN RECOVERING SOME OBJECTS.

ONE CREW MEMBER'S WATCH, WHICH HAD STOPPED AT THE TIME OF THE SHIPWRECK, WAS AUCTIONED OFF FOR OVER $169,000.

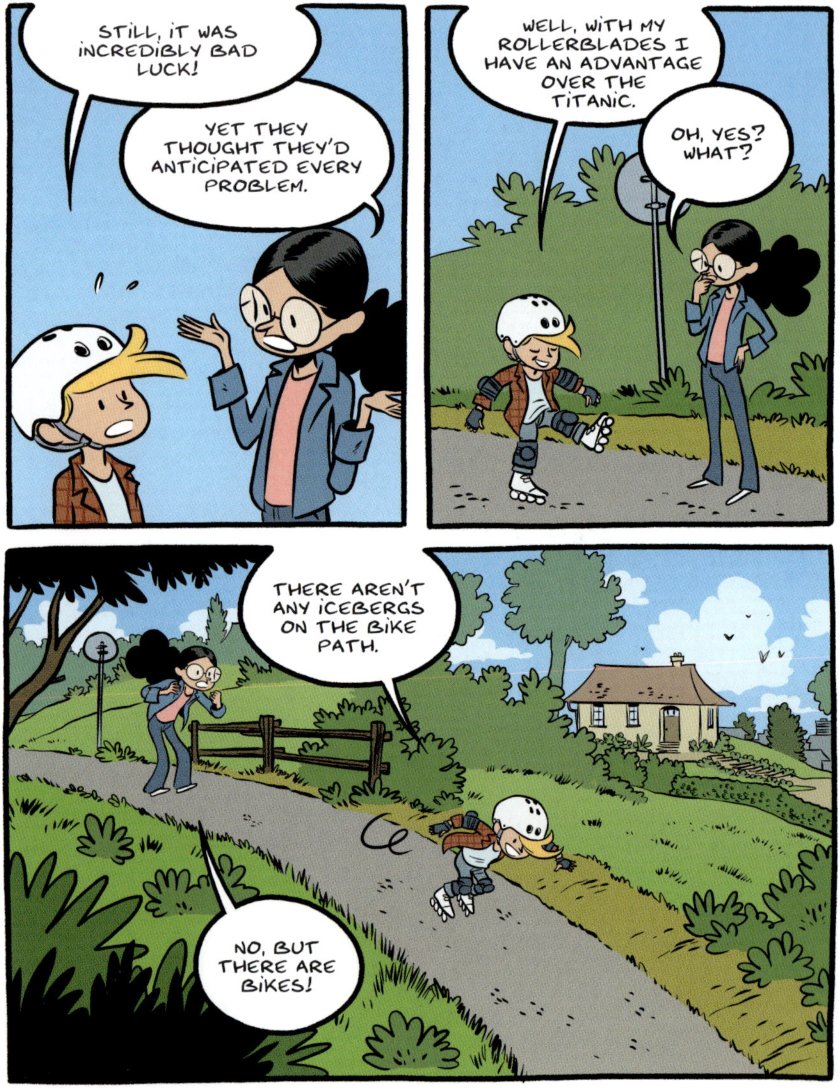

THERE AREN'T ANY ICEBERGS ON THE BIKE PATH.

NO, BUT THERE ARE BIKES!

And there's more...

Some People Who Made History

Edward John Smith
(1850-1912)

In 1912, Smith was the White Star Line's most experienced and respected captain. The voyage of the Titanic was the crowning achievement of his career, and he was considering retirement afterwards. Already in bed for the night, he was not in charge when the ship struck the iceberg. He recorded the damage, ordered distress signals fired, and gave the order to evacuate. Some witnesses claimed he killed himself, others that he jumped into the water to save a baby.

Thomas Andrews
(1873-1912)

A British naval architect, Andrews designed the Titanic as well as the Olympic and the Britannic. He and his entire team went on the Titanic's inaugural journey to make note of potential flaws. After the Titanic struck the iceberg, he realized the ship would sink and asked the captain to order the evacuation. Andrews took an active part in this, leading passengers towards the lifeboats. Last seen in the smoking room, he disappeared in the shipwreck.

Margaret Brown

(1867-1932)

Born into a poor family, Margaret "Molly" Brown and her husband, James, made a fortune thanks to the discovery of gold mines. Separated from her husband in 1909, Molly then traveled around the world and got on the Titanic to return home after a stay in Europe. Evacuating in lifeboat No. 6, she opposed the quartermaster, who refused to rescue other castaways for fear of capsizing. After the tragedy, she helped create the survivors' committee. Her story was retold on film.

Millvina Dean

(1912-2009)

Two months old when she came on board the Titanic with her family in third class, Millvina Dean was the youngest passenger. She was evacuated during the shipwreck on a lifeboat with her mother and brother according to the principle of "women and children first," but her father vanished in the catastrophe. Even though she had no memory of the event, she became a symbol of the survivors.
When she died in 2009 at the age of 97, the last witness of the tragedy was gone.

MAP OF THE TITANIC

DISTRIBUTION OF THE PASSENGERS

First Class

Second Class

Third Class

Crew

FACILITIES AND RECREATION AREAS

1 Squash Court
2 Pool
3 Turkish Baths
4 Gymnasium
5 Reception Room
6 Library
7 Smoking rooms

Supplies

Engines and coal supply

20,000 bottles of beer
1,500 bottles of wine,
8,000 cigars,
40 tons of potatoes
75,000 pounds of meat...

The three first smokestacks vented the smoke from the boilers; the fourth provided ventilation.

LENGTH: 882.5 feet
WIDTH: 92.5 feet
SPEED: 24 mph
WEIGHT: 46,328 tons

Bridge: the place where the ship is steered from.

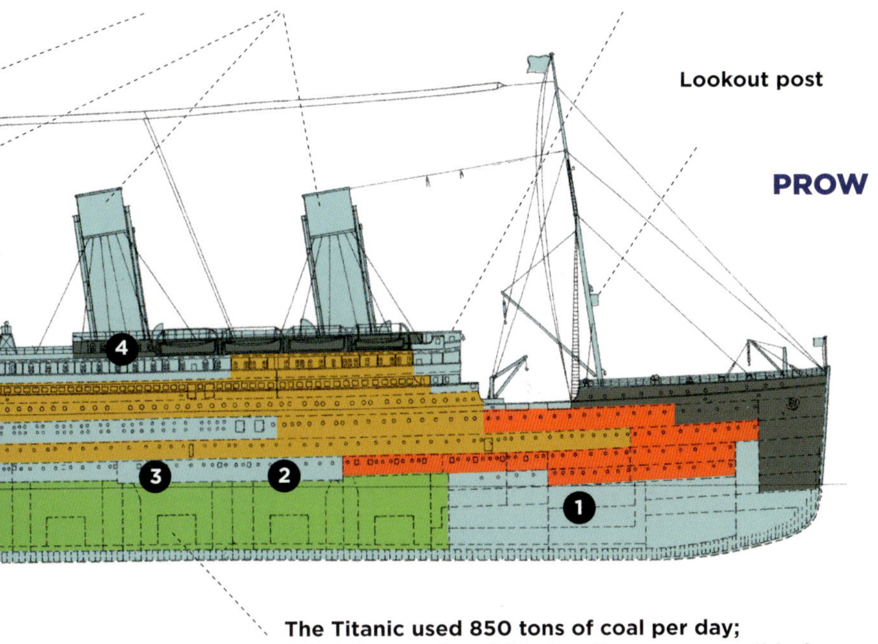

The Titanic used 850 tons of coal per day; 170 "trimmers" and "stokers" were responsible for continuously feeding the 29 boilers.

Stories and Legends About the Titanic

THE FAMED TITANIC WRECKAGE

As early as 1913, numerous projects were devised to raise the remains, from electromagnets to ping pong balls! They still had to find the wreck, but no one succeeded in doing so, not even The Walt Disney Company, which spent a fortune on investigations. **It would take until 1985 to discover it** and for it to be explored and documented. Wealthy tourists can even get near the wreckage for $125,000! But the remains are being devoured by a bacterium and it's expected to vanish between 2025 and 2050.

Other ships have surpassed the Titanic. The biggest modern ocean liner is the Symphony of the Seas, a ship built in France, which can transport **6,780 passengers** and is **1,184 feet** long, some 301 feet longer than the Titanic. In addition, the shipwrecks of two other ships have claimed more lives than the Titanic: the **Doña Paz** from the Philippines in 1987 (at least 1,565 deaths) and the **Joola** from Gambia in 2002 (about 2,000 deaths).

LITERARY PREMONITIONS

Twenty years before the tragedy of the Titanic, British writer **William Thomas Stead** published a short story called, "From the Old World to the New." The story was set on a White Star Line ship commanded by Edward Smith (the company and captain of the future Titanic), who saved the survivors of another ship that had collided with an iceberg. The writer died in 1912 - on the Titanic! Another writer, the American **Morgan Robertson**, wrote a novel entitled Futility, in which he told the story of the shipwreck of the Titan, the largest ocean liner of its time, after it struck an iceberg—fourteen years before the event!

MULTIPLE SHIPWRECK SURVIVOR

Violet Constance Jessop, a British maritime nurse, was on the **OLYMPIC** in 1911 when it crashed: its hull was damaged when it collided with another ship. Jessop next worked on the **TITANIC**, where she was saved on a lifeboat after it sank. Finally, in 1916, she was on assignment aboard the **Britannic** during World War I when it was sunk once again, she was saved, as were most of the passengers on that ship.

Timeline

1907 — Plans for the Titanic developed for the White Star Line

1909-1912 — Titanic built in Belfast, Ireland

1935 — The Olympic makes its last voyage.

1985 — The wreck of the Titanic identified at a depth of 12,536 feet.

1994 — RMS Titanic recognized as the only company authorized to salvage items from the shipwreck.

1997 — James Cameron's film, *Titanic*, premiered. It was the biggest global success in film for 13 years.

April 10, 1912
The Titanic leaves the port of Southampton in England.

April 14, 1912
Shipwreck of the Titanic.

May 1912
The first movie, *Saved from the Titanic*, filmed with survivor Dorothy Gibson.

1934
Construction of the Queen Mary, the first ocean liner to exceed 984 feet in length.

2009
Death of Millvina Dean, the last survivor of the shipwreck.

2013
An Australian billionaire unveils plans to rebuild the Titanic for tourists to sail on.

WATCH OUT FOR PAPERCUTZ™

Hello and welcome to the third volume of the triple-packed MAGICAL HISTORY TOUR! This series has three comics per book, all about people and history - in this case, about Gandhi, the Vikings, and the Titanic.

MAGICAL HISTORY TOUR is such a delightful book! Each story begins with Annie and Nico in the modern-day, doing modern-day things. In the first story in this book, Nico is running away from a bully that took his candy. In the second story, Annie and Nico are playing on the beach. And in the third story, Nico is getting ready to rollerskate down a hill.

This shows that Annie and Nico are peers for you, the reader. And it shows how people and history can relate to everything! History repeats itself and history can teach you how to change the future. If you wear kneepads, then you're less likely to hurt your knees when you rollerskate down that big hill. If you wear a helmet, you protect your head. You are benefiting from your own past, and from history itself, when you strap on that helmet and those kneepads. When you report a bully to a teacher, you are using a system that was built in response to previous problems with bullying. It may be imperfect, but you are using it and you and your family can give feedback for improvement for future kids too!

At the end of every comic - spoiler, Annie and Nico reenter the modern world. The opening is concluded - Nico rolls down that hill, with a little more knowledge. He applies the past to his present-day and moves into the future.

Have you ever learned something in class, and then used your knowledge?

And if you're interested in learning more, keep an eye out for MAGICAL HISTORY TOUR! Plus, if you like animals, you should check out JACKSON'S WILDER ADVENTURES! It's educational, but focuses on a boy named Jackson and his best friend, Irwin the Thylacine, as they learn about cool animals.

Thank you and we'll see you on the next magical (book) tour!

Jackson's Wilder Adventures

STAY IN TOUCH!

EMAIL:	**contact@papercutz.com**
WEB:	**www.papercutz.com**
TWITTER:	**@papercutzgn**
INSTAGRAM:	**@papercutzgn**
FACEBOOK:	**PAPERCUTZGRAPHICNOVELS**
FANMAIL:	**8838 SW 129 St. Miami. FL. 33176**

Go to papercutz.com and sign up for the free Papercutz e-newsletter!

YAHGZ™

BY ART BALTAZAR

JOIN CRAYBI CRAYNOBI AND HIS SON, CRAYSKI CRAYNOBI, THE FUTURE CHOSEN ONE WITH THE CHOSEN NOSE, AS WELL AS THEIR MANY FRIENDS AND ALLIES LIKE WEEZERD THE WISE WIZARD, AS THEY ADVENTURE THROUGH MYTHICAL LANDS TO TRY TO SAVE THE CITY OF YAHGZ AND ITS PEOPLE, THE YAHGEEZ. BUT ARE CRAYBI AND CRAYSKI ENOUGH TO FACE THE GIANT GREEN GORILLA? OR EVEN BIGGER FOES AS THEY FORD A RIVER OF MUD, OR ENTER THE LAND OF ASHES? CRAYBI AND CRAYSKI WILL NEED THEIR WITS AND SOME HELPFUL ALLIES TO HELP EVERYONE. FIND OUT HOW THEY SAVE YAHGZ IN THIS ZANY NEW GRAPHIC NOVEL SERIES BY WORLD-FAMOUS CARTOONIST ART BALTAZAR!

PAPERCUTZ™

WHERE WILL THE MAGICAL HISTORY TOUR BRING ANNIE AND NICO NEXT?

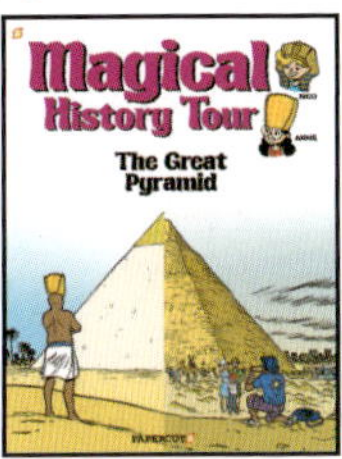

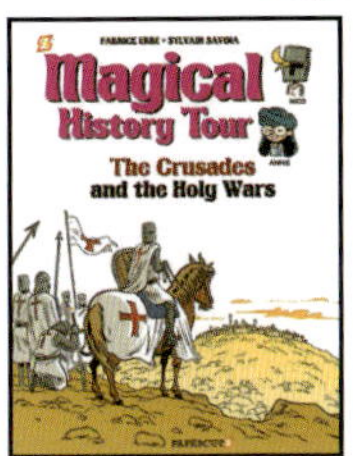

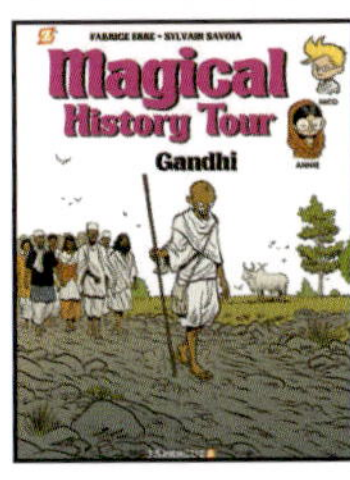

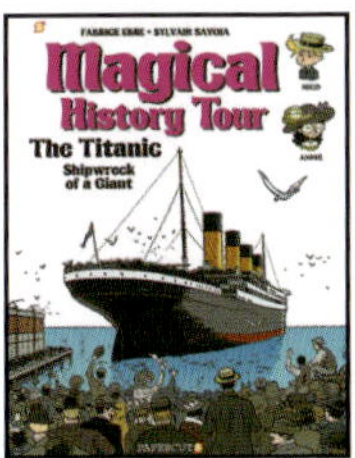

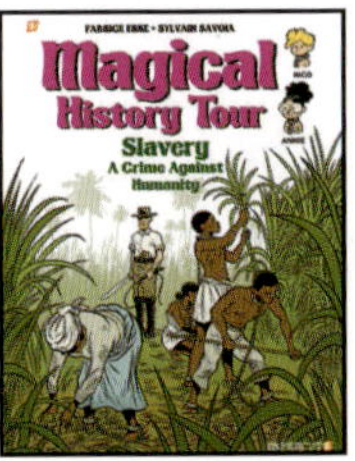

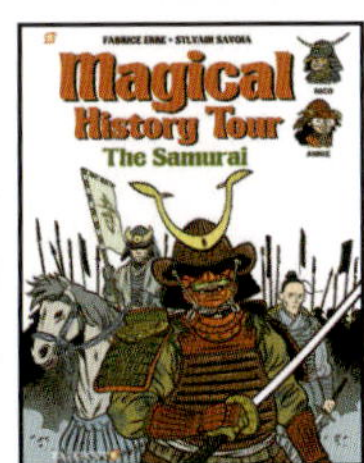

Available wherever books are sold.

Fabrice Erre has a Ph.D. in History and teaches Geography and History at the *Lycée Jean Jaures* near Montpellier, France. He has written a thesis on the satirical press, writes the blog *Une anne au lycée (A Year in High School)* on the website of *Le Monde*, one of France's top national newspapers, and has published several comics.

Sylvain Savoia draws the *Marzi* series, which tells the history of Poland as seen through the eyes of a child. He has also drawn *Les Esclaves oubliés de Tromelin (The Forgotten Slaves of Tromelin)*, which won the *Academie de Marine de Paris* prize.